NORTH MACEDONIA
TRAVEL GUIDE

Discover the Wonders of Skopje, Pelagonia, Vardar, Southwestern, and Eastern Regions.

Frattin Z. Daniele

TABLE OF CONTENTS

CHAPTER TEN 160

IMPORTANT NOTICE
While this guide is an invaluable resource for navigating and discovering NORTH MACEDONIA!, it should not be considered a substitute for professional advice or official information provided by relevant authorities. Travelers are urged to familiarize themselves with and adhere to local regulations, guidelines, and safety recommendations.

Frattin Z. Daniele

CHAPTER ONE

WELCOME TO NORTH MACEDONIA

Welcome to North Macedonia, a country where ancient history meets modern vibrancy, and natural beauty blends seamlessly with rich cultural traditions. Nestled in the heart of the Balkan Peninsula, North Macedonia offers an extraordinary journey through time, from its prehistoric heritage and classical antiquity to the diverse influences of the Byzantine, Ottoman, and modern eras. This guidebook serves as your gateway to discovering the many facets of this fascinating nation.

North Macedonia is a land of striking contrasts. The capital city, Skopje, epitomizes this blend, with its eclectic mix of classical and contemporary architecture, vibrant street life, and an array of cultural institutions. Wander through the historic Old Bazaar, one of the largest and most well-preserved marketplaces in the Balkans, where the past and present converge in a lively tapestry of commerce, cuisine, and craftsmanship. Marvel at the modernist marvels of the city center, punctuated by monumental sculptures and neoclassical facades that narrate the country's storied past.

Beyond the urban hustle, North Macedonia's natural landscapes beckon with their untouched beauty. The breathtaking Lake Ohrid, one of Europe's oldest and deepest lakes, is a UNESCO World Heritage site, offering crystal-clear waters and a backdrop of majestic mountains. Here, you can explore the ancient city of Ohrid, often referred to as the "Jerusalem of the Balkans," with its wealth of Byzantine churches, frescoes, and the iconic Samuel's Fortress overlooking the lake. The tranquil shores and serene beauty make it a perfect retreat for relaxation and exploration.

Venture further into the countryside, and you'll find the lush valleys and rugged peaks of the Mavrovo and Pelister National Parks. These protected areas are havens for outdoor enthusiasts, providing opportunities for hiking, skiing, and wildlife watching. The diverse flora and fauna, coupled with dramatic landscapes, offer an immersive experience in nature's splendor. The pristine environment and traditional mountain villages add to the charm, inviting visitors to experience a slower, more contemplative pace of life.

North Macedonia's rich cultural tapestry is woven from its multiethnic heritage. The country is home to a harmonious blend of Macedonians, Albanians, Turks, Roma, Serbs, and Vlachs, each contributing to the vibrant cultural mosaic. This diversity is reflected in the nation's music, dance, festivals, and culinary traditions. The traditional Macedonian cuisine, characterized by its hearty and flavorful dishes, offers a culinary journey that is both exotic and familiar, with influences from Mediterranean, Middle Eastern, and Balkan kitchens.

Festivals and celebrations are integral to North Macedonian culture, with events such as the Ohrid Summer Festival, the Strumica Carnival, and the Galichnik Wedding Festival offering colorful and immersive experiences. These festivities provide a window into the local customs, folklore, and communal spirit that define the nation's identity.

As you embark on your journey through North Macedonia, you will be welcomed with warm hospitality and genuine friendliness. The locals, known for their generosity and openness, are eager to share their traditions, stories, and the beauty of their homeland with visitors. Whether you are exploring bustling markets, tranquil lakesides, or ancient ruins, you will find that every corner of North Macedonia has a story to tell and a unique experience to offer.

This guidebook aims to provide you with all the essential information and insider tips needed to explore North Macedonia comprehensively. From practical travel advice to detailed cultural insights, it is designed to be your trusted companion as you uncover the wonders of this captivating country. Welcome to North Macedonia, where every journey is an adventure and every moment is a discovery.

Brief History of North Macedonia

The history of North Macedonia is a rich tapestry woven from various cultural, political, and social influences, spanning millennia. This narrative begins in prehistoric times, with evidence of human settlements dating back to the Neolithic period. Archaeological findings such as those at the sites of Tumba Madzhari and Stobi reveal the early inhabitants' sophisticated craftsmanship and societal organization.

The region's significance grew during classical antiquity as it became part of the ancient kingdom of Paeonia. However, its prominence truly soared with the rise of the Kingdom of Macedon. Under the leadership of Philip II and his son Alexander the Great, Macedon expanded its territory and influence, creating one of the most formidable empires in history. The legacy of Alexander's conquests spread Hellenistic culture far beyond its borders, leaving an indelible mark on the ancient world.

Following the decline of the Macedonian empire, the region fell under Roman rule in the 2nd century BCE. It was incorporated into the Roman province of Macedonia, becoming an integral part of the expansive Roman Empire. During this period, many cities, including Scupi (modern-day Skopje) and Heraclea Lyncestis (near Bitola), flourished as important centers of trade and culture. The remnants of Roman architecture and infrastructure, such as roads, theaters, and baths, can still be seen today, providing a window into the area's vibrant past.

With the division of the Roman Empire in the 4th century CE, the territory of modern-day North Macedonia became part of the Byzantine Empire. This era saw the spread of Christianity, which profoundly influenced the region's cultural and religious landscape. Numerous churches and monasteries were established, many of which still stand as testaments to Byzantine art and architecture.

The medieval period brought new dynamics as Slavic tribes settled in the Balkans during the 6th and 7th centuries. They gradually assimilated with the local population, laying the foundation for the formation of the Slavic Macedonian identity. The rise of the Bulgarian and Serbian empires further shaped the region, as it oscillated between their spheres of influence.

The Ottoman Empire's conquest of the Balkans in the late 14th century ushered in a period of significant change. For over five centuries, the region was under Ottoman rule, profoundly impacting its demographic, cultural, and architectural fabric. The introduction of Islam and the construction of mosques, baths, and bazaars added new layers to the multicultural mosaic. Despite this dominance, the local population maintained its distinct cultural identity, expressed through language, traditions, and resistance movements.

The decline of the Ottoman Empire in the 19th century ignited national awakenings across the Balkans. The struggle for independence culminated in the early 20th century, with the Balkan Wars and World War I reshaping the region's political landscape. After the dissolution of the Ottoman Empire, the territory of modern North Macedonia was incorporated into the Kingdom of Serbs, Croats, and Slovenes, later known as Yugoslavia.

World War II brought further upheaval, with the region becoming a battleground for various factions. In the aftermath, North Macedonia emerged as one of the six republics of the Socialist Federal Republic of Yugoslavia. This period saw significant industrialization, urbanization, and the promotion of Macedonian cultural identity. The republic enjoyed a degree of autonomy, yet remained closely tied to the central Yugoslav government.

The dissolution of Yugoslavia in the early 1990s paved the way for North Macedonia's declaration of independence in 1991. However, the journey to full international recognition was fraught with challenges, particularly the naming dispute with Greece. This issue was resolved in 2019 with the Prespa Agreement, officially renaming the country the Republic of North Macedonia.

Today, North Macedonia stands as a sovereign nation, a member of international organizations like the United Nations and NATO, and a candidate for European Union membership. Its history is a testament to resilience and adaptability, reflecting a unique blend of influences that have shaped its identity over the centuries.

Geographical Backgrounds And Climatic Factors

North Macedonia, a landlocked country in the heart of the Balkan Peninsula, boasts a diverse geographical landscape that plays a crucial role in shaping its climate and natural beauty. Covering an area of approximately 25,700 square kilometers, it shares borders with Kosovo to the northwest, Serbia to the north, Bulgaria to the east, Greece to the south, and Albania to the west. The country's terrain is predominantly mountainous, interspersed with deep valleys, fertile plains, and numerous rivers and lakes.

The central and western regions of North Macedonia are dominated by the Dinaric Alps and the Šar Mountains, which extend into neighboring Kosovo and Albania. These rugged mountain ranges, including the highest peak, Mount Korab, standing at 2,764 meters, offer stunning vistas and a haven for outdoor enthusiasts. The eastern part of the country is characterized by the Osogovo-Belasica mountain chain, which features gentler slopes and rich biodiversity.

Interspersed among these mountains are several significant valleys and basins, such as the Vardar River Valley, which is the country's largest and most important. The Vardar River, the longest river in North Macedonia, flows from the northwest to the southeast, eventually emptying into the Aegean Sea. This river valley is a vital corridor for transportation and commerce, as well as a fertile agricultural region supporting a variety of crops and vineyards.

One of North Macedonia's most renowned natural features is its collection of lakes. Lake Ohrid, one of Europe's oldest and deepest lakes, straddles the border with Albania and is a UNESCO World Heritage site. Its crystal-clear waters and diverse ecosystem are a focal point for tourism and environmental conservation. Lake Prespa, shared with Albania and Greece, and Lake Dojran, shared with Greece, are also significant bodies of water, each contributing to the region's ecological and economic landscape.

The country's varied topography influences its climate, which can be categorized as transitional between Mediterranean and continental. This results in diverse climatic conditions across different regions. In general, North Macedonia experiences four distinct seasons: spring, summer, autumn, and winter.

The Vardar River Valley and the central plains typically have a moderate continental climate, characterized by hot, dry summers and cold, wet winters. Average summer temperatures in these areas can reach 30°C (86°F) or higher, while winter temperatures often drop below freezing, with occasional snowfall.

In contrast, the mountainous regions, particularly the western and northern parts, experience a more alpine climate. Summers are cooler and pleasant, making these areas popular for hiking and outdoor activities. Winters in the mountains are cold and snowy, providing excellent conditions for winter sports such as skiing and snowboarding. The Šar Mountains and Mavrovo National Park are particularly known for their winter recreational facilities.

The southern regions, including the areas around Lake Ohrid and the southeastern border with Greece, enjoy a more Mediterranean-influenced climate. Here, summers are long, hot, and dry, while winters are milder and wetter compared to the rest of the country. The temperate climate around Lake Ohrid makes it a year-round destination for tourists, with warm summers perfect for swimming and boating, and mild winters suitable for cultural exploration.

Rainfall in North Macedonia varies significantly by region and season. The western mountainous areas receive the highest precipitation, particularly during the spring and autumn months. The central and eastern parts of the country, including the Vardar River Valley, tend to be drier, with most rainfall occurring in late spring and early autumn.

Understanding North Macedonia's geographical diversity and climatic conditions is essential for appreciating its natural beauty and planning a visit. The interplay of mountains, valleys, rivers, and lakes creates a landscape that is both picturesque and varied, offering a wide range of activities and experiences throughout the year.

Whether you're drawn to the serene lakes, rugged mountains, or fertile valleys, North Macedonia's geography and climate ensure a unique and enriching journey.

CHAPTER TWO

PLANNING YOUR TRIP TO North Macedonia

Planning a trip to North Macedonia involves thoughtful consideration of various practical aspects to ensure a smooth and enjoyable experience. From understanding visa requirements to choosing the best time to visit, this guide will provide you with all the essential information you need for a well-prepared journey.

Visa and Entry Requirements

North Macedonia is accessible to travelers from many countries without the need for a visa for short stays. Citizens of the European Union, the United States, Canada, Australia, and several other nations can enter the country visa-free for up to 90 days within a six-month period. However, it is advisable to check the latest entry requirements with your local North Macedonian embassy or consulate, as regulations may change. Ensure your passport is valid for at least six months beyond your planned departure date.

Best Time to Visit

The optimal time to visit North Macedonia depends on your interests and preferred activities. The country experiences four distinct seasons, each offering unique experiences:

Spring (April to June): This season is ideal for outdoor activities such as hiking, cycling, and exploring historical sites. The weather is mild, and the landscapes are lush and blooming.

Summer (July to September): Warm and sunny, summer is perfect for enjoying the lakes, particularly Lake Ohrid, and attending festivals. However, be prepared for higher temperatures in the central and southern regions.

Autumn (October to November): With cooler temperatures and vibrant foliage, autumn is a great time for sightseeing and nature walks. It is also the harvest season, providing opportunities to sample local produce.
Winter (December to March): If you enjoy winter sports, the mountainous regions offer excellent skiing and snowboarding conditions. The festive atmosphere around the holidays adds a special charm to your visit.

Transportation
North Macedonia has a well-developed transportation network that makes it easy to explore the country. The main international gateway is Skopje Alexander the Great Airport, with flights connecting to major European cities. Ohrid St. Paul the Apostle Airport also serves as a convenient entry point for visitors heading to the southwestern part of the country.

For domestic travel, the bus network is extensive and reliable, connecting major cities and towns. Trains offer an alternative mode of transportation, though the rail network is more limited. Car rental is a popular option for those who prefer the flexibility of self-driving, and the country's compact size makes it easy to explore by car.

Accommodation
North Macedonia offers a wide range of accommodation options to suit all budgets and preferences. From luxury hotels and boutique guesthouses to budget hostels and charming bed-and-breakfasts, you'll find suitable lodging in major cities and tourist areas. For a unique experience, consider staying in traditional village accommodations or eco-friendly lodges in rural areas.

Currency and Banking
The official currency of North Macedonia is the Macedonian denar (MKD). ATMs are widely available in cities and towns, and credit cards are commonly accepted in hotels, restaurants, and larger shops. It's advisable to carry some cash for smaller establishments and markets. Currency exchange services are readily available at banks, exchange offices, and airports.

Health and Safety
North Macedonia is generally a safe destination for travelers. Medical facilities are available in major cities, and pharmacies are well-stocked. It's recommended to have travel insurance that covers medical expenses and emergencies. While tap water is generally safe to drink in urban areas, bottled water is advisable in rural regions.

Local Customs and Etiquette

Familiarizing yourself with local customs and etiquette will enhance your travel experience. Macedonians are known for their hospitality and friendliness. When greeting someone, a handshake is common, and it's polite to use formal titles unless invited to do otherwise. Dress modestly when visiting religious sites and always ask for permission before taking photographs of people or private property.

Sustainable and Responsible Travel

North Macedonia is committed to sustainable tourism practices. Support local communities by purchasing locally-made products and dining at family-owned restaurants. Be mindful of your environmental impact by minimizing waste, conserving water, and respecting natural habitats.

By carefully planning your trip and considering these practical aspects, you will be well-prepared to enjoy all that North Macedonia has to offer. This fascinating country, with its rich history, diverse landscapes, and warm hospitality, promises an unforgettable travel experience.

Right Time to Visit

Choosing the best time to visit North Macedonia depends largely on your interests and what you hope to experience during your trip. The country's diverse climate offers unique attractions and activities throughout the year, making it a versatile destination for all seasons.

Spring (April to June)

Spring is a delightful time to visit North Macedonia. As the country emerges from the winter chill, the landscapes burst into vibrant colors with blooming flowers and lush greenery. This season is ideal for outdoor activities such as hiking, cycling, and exploring historical sites. The temperatures are mild, typically ranging from 15°C to 25°C (59°F to 77°F), providing comfortable conditions for sightseeing and nature walks. Spring is also less crowded, offering a more peaceful experience at popular tourist spots like Lake Ohrid and the Matka Canyon.

Summer (July to September)

Summer is the peak tourist season in North Macedonia, particularly in July and August. During these months, the weather is warm and sunny, with temperatures often reaching 30°C (86°F) or higher, especially in the central and southern regions. This is the perfect time for enjoying the country's beautiful lakes, such as Lake Ohrid and Lake Prespa, where you can swim, boat, and partake in various water sports. The summer months also feature numerous cultural events and festivals, including the renowned Ohrid Summer Festival, which showcases music, theater, and dance performances. However, be prepared for larger crowds and higher accommodation prices.

Autumn (October to November)

Autumn is a fantastic time to visit North Macedonia if you prefer cooler temperatures and fewer tourists. The weather is generally pleasant, with temperatures ranging from 10°C to 20°C (50°F to 68°F), making it ideal for sightseeing and outdoor activities. The countryside transforms into a stunning palette of reds, oranges, and yellows, providing a picturesque backdrop for hikes and scenic drives. This season is also harvest time, offering visitors the chance to sample fresh local produce and participate in traditional agricultural festivals. Autumn is perfect for exploring vineyards and tasting North Macedonia's renowned wines.

Winter (December to March)

Winter in North Macedonia brings a different kind of charm, particularly for those who enjoy winter sports. The mountainous regions, especially the Šar Mountains and Mavrovo National Park, offer excellent conditions for skiing, snowboarding, and other snow-related activities. The temperatures in these areas can drop significantly, often below freezing, creating a winter wonderland. In the cities, the festive atmosphere during the holiday season adds to the appeal, with Christmas markets, local celebrations, and traditional foods. While the weather can be cold, the cultural richness and the warmth of the local hospitality make winter an inviting time to visit.

Considerations for Specific Interests

Wildlife and Nature Enthusiasts: Spring and autumn are ideal for observing the diverse flora and fauna in North Macedonia's national parks, such as Pelister and Galichica. These seasons offer comfortable temperatures and vibrant natural settings.

Cultural Explorers: Summer provides the most opportunities to experience North Macedonia's cultural festivals and events. However, spring and autumn also offer rich cultural experiences without the peak season crowds.

Budget Travelers: For those looking to travel on a budget, the shoulder seasons of spring and autumn often provide lower accommodation rates and fewer tourists, allowing for a more affordable and relaxed trip.

Visa and Entry Requirements

Understanding the visa and entry requirements for North Macedonia is essential for planning a smooth and hassle-free trip to this Balkan nation. Whether you're traveling for tourism, business, or other purposes, knowing the regulations and necessary documentation will ensure a seamless entry into the country.

Visa-Free Entry

North Macedonia allows visa-free entry for citizens of many countries for short stays of up to 90 days within a six-month period. Travelers from the European Union (EU), the United States, Canada, Australia, and several other countries fall under this category. This leniency makes North Macedonia accessible to a wide range of international visitors without the need for prior visa arrangements.

Entry Requirements

To enter North Macedonia as a visa-free traveler, you must possess a valid passport with an expiration date that extends at least six months beyond your intended departure from the country. It's essential to ensure that your passport meets these validity requirements to avoid any issues upon arrival.

Extensions and Long-Term Stays

If you plan to stay in North Macedonia for longer than the permitted 90 days within a six-month period or for purposes other than tourism (such as work or study), you may need to apply for a visa or other specific permits. Requirements for long-term stays vary depending on your nationality and the purpose of your visit. It's advisable to contact the nearest North Macedonian embassy or consulate well in advance to obtain the necessary information and guidance for your specific circumstances.

Visa Requirements for Specific Countries

While citizens of many countries enjoy visa-free entry to North Macedonia, some nationalities do require a visa. Travelers from countries not included in the visa-free regime should check with the nearest North Macedonian embassy or consulate to determine the specific visa requirements and application procedures. Visa applications typically require a completed application form, passport photos, proof of accommodation, travel itinerary, proof of sufficient funds, and possibly additional documents depending on the purpose of the visit.

Border Crossings and Exit Requirements
When entering North Macedonia, travelers may be required to fill out an arrival form, which includes basic information about their stay. It's important to complete this form accurately and keep it with your passport until departure. When leaving North Macedonia, ensure you have all necessary documents, including a valid passport and any exit forms provided by immigration authorities.

Traveling with Minors
If you are traveling with minors (under 18 years old), additional documentation may be required, such as birth certificates and parental consent forms. These requirements can vary depending on the child's nationality and accompanying adults. Check with the North Macedonian embassy or consulate for specific details before traveling.

Health and Insurance Considerations
While not directly related to visa requirements, it is advisable to have travel insurance that covers medical expenses and emergencies during your stay in North Macedonia. Medical facilities are generally good in major cities, but having insurance provides peace of mind in case of unexpected health issues.

Stay Informed and Prepared

Visa and entry requirements can change, so it's crucial to stay informed about any updates or amendments to regulations before your trip. The Ministry of Foreign Affairs of North Macedonia and its diplomatic missions abroad are reliable sources of information regarding visa policies and entry requirements.

Travel Insurance

Travel insurance is an essential aspect of planning a trip to North Macedonia, offering financial protection and peace of mind in case of unforeseen events. Whether you're exploring historic sites, hiking in national parks, or enjoying the local cuisine, having adequate travel insurance ensures that you're prepared for any potential emergencies or disruptions during your journey.

Importance of Travel Insurance

Travel insurance provides coverage for a range of situations that could affect your trip, including medical emergencies, trip cancellations or interruptions, lost or delayed baggage, and emergency evacuation. In North Macedonia, as in any foreign country, unexpected medical expenses can be costly, and having insurance can help mitigate these expenses and ensure you receive necessary medical treatment without financial strain.

Medical Coverage

When traveling to North Macedonia, it's advisable to have travel insurance that includes comprehensive medical coverage. This coverage should encompass medical treatment for illnesses or injuries sustained during your trip, including hospitalization, doctor visits, prescription medications, and emergency medical evacuation if necessary. Verify that your insurance policy covers medical expenses incurred abroad and offers a 24-hour emergency assistance hotline for immediate support.

Trip Cancellation and Interruption

Travel insurance can reimburse you for prepaid and non-refundable expenses if your trip is canceled or interrupted due to unforeseen circumstances, such as illness, injury, or a family emergency. This coverage can include expenses related to flights, accommodations, and activities that you are unable to use due to unexpected events.

Baggage and Personal Belongings

Insurance for lost, stolen, or damaged baggage provides reimbursement for the value of your belongings if they are lost or damaged during your trip. This coverage typically extends to personal items such as clothing, electronics, and travel documents. Keep receipts and documentation for valuable items to facilitate the claims process in case of loss or damage.

Emergency Evacuation and Repatriation

In the event of a medical emergency or natural disaster, travel insurance may cover the cost of emergency evacuation to the nearest adequate medical facility or repatriation to your home country for further medical treatment. This coverage ensures that you receive appropriate medical care and transportation without incurring substantial out-of-pocket expenses.

Activities and Sports Coverage

If you plan to engage in adventure activities or sports while in North Macedonia, such as skiing, hiking, or water sports, ensure that your travel insurance policy includes coverage for these activities. Some insurers offer specific policies tailored to adventure travelers, providing additional coverage for potential risks associated with high-risk activities.

Policy Considerations

Before purchasing travel insurance for North Macedonia, carefully review the policy details, including coverage limits, exclusions, deductibles, and the claims process. Compare different insurance providers to find a policy that meets your specific needs and provides adequate coverage for the duration and activities of your trip.

Obtaining Travel Insurance

Travel insurance can be purchased from insurance companies, travel agencies, or online platforms specializing in travel insurance. Consider factors such as the reputation of the insurer, customer reviews, and the comprehensiveness of the coverage offered. Some credit card companies also provide travel insurance as a cardholder benefit, so check if your credit card includes travel insurance and its coverage details.

Language and communication

Language plays a pivotal role in cultural identity and communication in North Macedonia, reflecting the country's diverse heritage and historical influences. Understanding the linguistic landscape and communication norms enhances the travel experience, facilitating meaningful interactions and immersive cultural exchanges.

Official Language

The official language of North Macedonia is Macedonian, a South Slavic language closely related to Bulgarian and Serbian. Macedonian uses the Cyrillic alphabet, which consists of 31 letters and is primarily used in official documents, signage, and formal communication. Learning a few basic phrases in Macedonian, such as greetings (zdravo), thank you (blagodaram), and please (vi molam), can greatly enhance communication and show respect for local customs.

Minority Languages

In addition to Macedonian, several minority languages are spoken across North Macedonia, reflecting the country's multicultural diversity. Albanian is the most widely spoken minority language and holds official status in areas where Albanians constitute a significant population, such as Tetovo and Gostivar. Other minority languages include Turkish, Serbian, Romani, and Bosnian, each contributing to the linguistic tapestry of the region.

English Proficiency

English is increasingly spoken and understood in urban areas, particularly among younger generations, professionals in the tourism industry, and those engaged in international business. In major cities like Skopje and Ohrid, as well as popular tourist destinations, many signs, menus, and tourist information materials are available in English. Visitors can typically expect to find English-speaking staff in hotels, restaurants, and tourist attractions, making it relatively easy to navigate and communicate in English during their stay.

Communication Tips

When communicating with locals in North Macedonia, approach interactions with politeness and respect. Using formal titles (gospodin for Mr. and gospođa for Mrs.) when addressing individuals you meet for the first time is considered courteous. Handshakes are a common greeting among both men and women. Personal space is valued, so maintain an appropriate distance during conversations.

Signage and Public Information

Public signage in North Macedonia is predominantly in Macedonian, using the Cyrillic script. In tourist areas and transportation hubs, signs may also be displayed in English and occasionally in Albanian or other minority languages. Maps, brochures, and information boards at tourist sites often provide multilingual information to accommodate international visitors.

Language Learning Opportunities

For travelers interested in delving deeper into Macedonian culture and language, language learning opportunities are available through language schools, cultural centers, and private tutors in major cities. These programs offer structured courses in Macedonian, as well as cultural immersion experiences to enhance language proficiency and understanding of local customs.

Nonverbal Communication

Nonverbal communication plays a significant role in interactions in North Macedonia. Maintaining eye contact during conversations demonstrates attentiveness and respect. Gestures such as nodding or shaking the head are commonly used to indicate agreement or disagreement. When visiting religious sites or participating in cultural events, observe and respect local customs regarding appropriate behavior and attire.

Currency and Banking

Understanding the currency and banking system in North Macedonia is essential for travelers seeking to navigate financial transactions smoothly during their visit. From currency exchange to banking services,

Official Currency

The official currency of North Macedonia is the Macedonian denar (MKD), denoted by the symbol ден. The denar is subdivided into 100 deni. Banknotes are available in denominations of 10, 50, 100, 500, 1000, 2000, and 5000 denars, while coins come in denominations of 1, 2, 5, 10, and 50 deni, as well as 1, 2, and 5 denars. When exchanging currency, ensure that you receive updated denominations, as older banknotes may still be in circulation.

Currency Exchange

Currency exchange services are widely available in North Macedonia, particularly in major cities, tourist areas, airports, and hotels. Banks, exchange offices (menjačnica), and authorized currency exchange booths offer competitive exchange rates for various foreign currencies, including US dollars (USD), euros (EUR), British pounds (GBP), and Swiss francs (CHF). It is advisable to compare rates and fees among different providers to obtain the best exchange value.

Using Credit Cards and ATMs

Credit cards such as Visa, MasterCard, and American Express are generally accepted in larger hotels, restaurants, shops, and car rental agencies in North Macedonia. However, smaller establishments and rural areas may prefer cash payments. ATMs (bankomati) are widespread in urban centers and tourist hubs, dispensing denars and often accepting major international debit and credit cards. Withdrawals may be subject to transaction fees, so check with your bank regarding international withdrawal charges and notify them of your travel plans to avoid any issues with card usage abroad.

Traveler's Checks and Foreign Currency

While traveler's checks are less commonly used today, some banks in North Macedonia may still accept them for exchange. However, they are not as convenient as debit or credit cards and may incur higher fees or unfavorable exchange rates. It's recommended to carry a small amount of denars for immediate expenses upon arrival and rely on credit cards or ATMs for additional cash needs.

Banking Hours and Services

Banking hours in North Macedonia typically run from Monday to Friday, from 8:00 AM to 4:00 PM, with some banks closing earlier on Fridays. In larger cities like Skopje and Ohrid, certain branches may offer extended hours and limited services on Saturdays. Banks provide a range of services, including currency exchange, money transfers, savings and checking accounts, and loans. English-speaking staff are available at many banks and can assist with basic banking transactions and inquiries.

Currency Regulations

There are no restrictions on the import or export of local or foreign currency when entering or leaving North Macedonia. Travelers are required to declare amounts exceeding 10,000 euros or its equivalent in other currencies at customs upon arrival or departure.

Tips for Currency and Banking

Exchange Rates: Monitor exchange rates before exchanging currency to maximize your funds.

ATM Usage: Use ATMs located in secure and well-lit areas to avoid potential security risks.

Currency Conversion: When using credit cards abroad, opt for transactions in the local currency (denars) rather than your home currency to avoid dynamic currency conversion fees.

Local Customs and Etiquette

Understanding and respecting local customs and etiquette is key to experiencing the warm hospitality and cultural richness of North Macedonia. As you explore this Balkan nation known for its historical landmarks, picturesque landscapes, and vibrant traditions, embracing local customs enhances interactions with residents and enriches your travel experience.

Greetings and Interactions

Greetings in North Macedonia are generally warm and respectful. When meeting someone for the first time, it is customary to shake hands, maintaining eye contact and offering a friendly smile. Use formal titles such as gospodin (Mr.) and gospođa (Mrs.) followed by the surname when addressing individuals you meet in formal settings. Personal space is valued, so maintain an appropriate distance during conversations.

Hospitality and Invitations

Hospitality is deeply ingrained in Macedonian culture, and guests are warmly welcomed into homes with generosity and sincerity. If invited to someone's home, it's polite to bring a small gift, such as flowers, chocolates, or wine. Accepting refreshments and meals graciously is customary, as refusing hospitality may be seen as impolite. Express appreciation for the host's generosity and engage in polite conversation during your visit.

Dining Etiquette

Dining in North Macedonia often involves hearty meals shared with family and friends. When dining out, wait to be seated by the host or hostess. It is courteous to wait until everyone is served before beginning to eat. During meals, engage in conversation but avoid controversial topics such as politics or sensitive historical issues. Compliment the meal to show appreciation for the host's efforts.

Dress Code and Modesty

North Macedonians generally dress conservatively, especially in rural areas and religious sites. When visiting churches, monasteries, or mosques, dress modestly, covering shoulders and knees. In urban centers like Skopje, Ohrid, and Bitola, casual attire is acceptable, though beachwear is appropriate only at beaches and pools.

Religious Respect

Religion holds significant importance in North Macedonia, with Orthodox Christianity being the predominant faith. Respect religious customs and practices, such as removing hats and maintaining quiet during prayers when visiting churches and monasteries.

Women are typically expected to cover their heads with a scarf or shawl when entering Orthodox churches.

Festivals and Celebrations

North Macedonia celebrates numerous cultural and religious festivals throughout the year, such as Orthodox Christian holidays, cultural music festivals, and local traditions like the Strumica Carnival. Participating in these events offers insight into Macedonian traditions, music, dance, and culinary delights. Respect local customs during festivities and seek permission before taking photographs, especially during religious ceremonies.

Language and Communication

While Macedonian is the official language, many North Macedonians also speak English, particularly in tourist areas and among the younger population. Learning a few basic phrases in Macedonian, such as hello (zdravo), thank you (blagodaram), and please (vi molam), shows respect for the local culture and facilitates interactions with residents who may not speak English fluently.

Tipping and Gratuities

Tipping is appreciated but not mandatory in North Macedonia. In restaurants, it is customary to round up the bill or leave a 10% to 15% tip for good service. Tipping taxi drivers, hotel staff, and tour guides is also appreciated for exceptional service.

Health and Safety

Ensuring your health and safety is paramount when visiting North Macedonia, a country renowned for its rich history, stunning landscapes, and warm hospitality. Familiarizing yourself with health precautions, emergency services, and safety guidelines enhances your travel experience, allowing you to explore this Balkan gem with confidence and peace of mind.

Health Precautions

North Macedonia maintains adequate medical facilities in major cities like Skopje, Bitola, and Ohrid, offering comprehensive healthcare services including hospitals, clinics, and pharmacies. While tap water is generally safe to drink in urban areas, it's advisable for travelers to consume bottled water in rural regions and smaller towns to avoid potential gastrointestinal issues. Visitors should consider obtaining travel insurance that covers medical expenses, including hospitalization and emergency evacuation if necessary.

Vaccinations

Before traveling to North Macedonia, ensure your routine vaccinations are up-to-date, including measles-mumps-rubella (MMR), diphtheria-tetanus-pertussis, varicella (chickenpox), polio, and influenza. Hepatitis A and B vaccinations are recommended for travelers anticipating contact with contaminated food or water. Consult with your healthcare provider or visit a travel clinic at least four to six weeks before departure to discuss additional vaccinations or health precautions based on your itinerary and personal health.

Medical Services and Emergencies

In the event of a medical emergency, dial 194 for ambulance services, operated by the Emergency Medicine Service. English-speaking operators are available, though it's beneficial to have a local or bilingual speaker assist during emergencies for effective communication. Hospitals and medical centers in North Macedonia provide quality care, but carrying copies of your travel insurance policy and relevant medical records can expedite treatment and administrative processes.

Safety and Security

North Macedonia is generally safe for travelers with low crime rates compared to many European countries. However, exercising standard precautions is advisable:

Street Safety: Exercise caution in crowded or unfamiliar areas, especially after dark. Keep valuables secure and be aware of your surroundings.

Natural Hazards: North Macedonia occasionally experiences earthquakes, particularly in seismic zones. Familiarize yourself with safety procedures and follow local authorities' instructions during seismic events.

Driving: If driving in North Macedonia, adhere to local traffic laws and regulations. Roads can be narrow and winding, particularly in rural areas, so drive cautiously and observe local driving customs.

Traveling Solo and Women's Safety
Solo travelers, including women, generally find North Macedonia to be a welcoming and safe destination. Standard precautions such as avoiding isolated areas at night and maintaining awareness in public places apply. Respect local customs and dress modestly when visiting religious sites or participating in cultural events.

Environmental Considerations
Promote environmental conservation by disposing of waste responsibly and minimizing plastic usage, particularly in national parks and protected areas. Respect wildlife and natural habitats during your travels to preserve North Macedonia's scenic beauty for future generations.

Emergency Contacts
Emergency Services: Ambulance: 194
Police: 192
Fire Department: 193

CHAPTER THREE

GETTING TO NORTH MACEDONIA

Traveling to North Macedonia is convenient with several transportation options available to international visitors. The country is served by two main airports: Skopje International Airport (SKP) and Ohrid St. Paul the Apostle Airport (OHD). Skopje Airport, located near the capital city, offers direct flights from major European hubs such as Vienna, Zurich, Istanbul, and London. Ohrid Airport provides seasonal flights from destinations across Europe.

For those arriving by land, North Macedonia is accessible via well-maintained road networks from neighboring countries such as Serbia, Kosovo, Albania, Bulgaria, and Greece. International bus services operate from cities like Belgrade, Sofia, and Thessaloniki, offering affordable and efficient travel options for regional visitors.

Travelers can also reach North Macedonia by train, with international rail connections from Serbia and Kosovo into Skopje. Whether by air, road, or rail, reaching North Macedonia is straightforward, providing access to its cultural treasures, natural wonders, and warm hospitality.

By Air

Traveling to North Macedonia by air offers convenient access to this Balkan gem, known for its rich history, scenic landscapes, and vibrant culture. The country is served by two main international airports:

Skopje International Airport (SKP)

Skopje Airport is the primary gateway to North Macedonia, located approximately 17 kilometers southeast of the capital city, Skopje. It operates direct flights to and from major European cities such as Vienna, Zurich, Istanbul, London, and several others. Airlines serving Skopje Airport include Turkish Airlines, Austrian Airlines, Wizz Air, and others, providing frequent connections for both business and leisure travelers.

Ohrid St. Paul the Apostle Airport (OHD)

Ohrid Airport, situated near the picturesque town of Ohrid in southwestern North Macedonia, offers seasonal flights from various European destinations. During the peak tourist season, Ohrid Airport welcomes direct flights from cities like Amsterdam, Brussels, Warsaw, and other major European hubs. Airlines operating seasonal services to Ohrid include Corendon Airlines, TUI Airways, and others, catering to travelers seeking to explore the cultural and natural wonders of Ohrid and its surroundings.

Airport Services and Transportation

Both Skopje and Ohrid airports offer modern facilities, including duty-free shops, restaurants, car rental services, and transportation options to city centers. Taxis and airport shuttles provide convenient transfers to downtown Skopje or Ohrid, with journey times varying depending on traffic conditions.

Travelers to North Macedonia can also explore additional flight options via nearby airports in neighboring countries, such as Thessaloniki International Airport (Greece) or Sofia Airport (Bulgaria), followed by a short overland journey into North Macedonia. Whether arriving for business or leisure, North Macedonia's international airports ensure seamless travel experiences, connecting visitors to the country's diverse attractions and warm hospitality.

By land

Traveling to North Macedonia by land offers a scenic and practical way to explore this culturally rich Balkan nation, renowned for its historical sites, natural beauty, and warm hospitality. The country is well-connected to its neighboring countries through an extensive network of roads and border crossings, facilitating convenient overland travel for visitors.

Road Networks and Border Crossings

North Macedonia shares borders with several countries, including Serbia, Kosovo, Albania, Bulgaria, and Greece. Major highways and well-maintained roads link North Macedonia to these neighboring nations, providing smooth and efficient travel routes for both private vehicles and international buses.

From Serbia and Kosovo

From Serbia, travelers can enter North Macedonia via the E75 highway, connecting Belgrade to Skopje. Border crossings such as Tabanovce are well-equipped for processing international travelers. Similarly, crossings from Kosovo, including the Blace crossing near Kumanovo, offer accessible routes into North Macedonia.

From Albania and Bulgaria

Travelers from Albania can reach North Macedonia via the E852 highway, with border crossings at Debar and Struga providing entry points. From Bulgaria, routes via the E871 and E79 highways lead to North Macedonia, with border crossings at Gyueshevo and Delchevo facilitating entry and exit.

From Greece

The E-75 highway connects Thessaloniki in Greece to North Macedonia, with border crossings such as Evzoni providing access. This route is popular for travelers visiting Skopje or continuing their journey to other parts of North Macedonia.

International Bus Services

International bus services operate regular routes between North Macedonia and neighboring countries, offering affordable and comfortable travel options for regional visitors. Buses depart from cities like Belgrade, Sofia, Tirana, and Pristina, providing convenient connections to Skopje and other major cities in North Macedonia.

Customs and Immigration

When crossing borders into North Macedonia, travelers are required to present valid travel documents, including passports and visas if necessary. Border procedures are generally straightforward, though it's advisable to check current entry requirements and any travel advisories before departure.

Traveling to North Macedonia by land offers a rewarding experience, combining scenic landscapes with convenient access to cultural and historical sites. Whether exploring ancient cities, hiking in national parks, or enjoying local cuisine, overland travel provides opportunities to immerse yourself in North Macedonia's diverse attractions and authentic hospitality.

By Train

Traveling to North Macedonia by train offers a unique and scenic journey through the Balkans, providing access to historical landmarks, picturesque landscapes, and cultural diversity. While North Macedonia's railway network is not as extensive as some European countries, it provides international connections that enhance travel options for visitors.

International Rail Connections

North Macedonia is primarily accessible by train from neighboring countries such as Serbia and Kosovo. The Belgrade-Skopje railway line connects Serbia's capital, Belgrade, to Skopje, North Macedonia's capital. This route offers a picturesque journey through mountainous terrain and historical regions, providing travelers with a memorable introduction to the country.

Train Services and Facilities

Trains traveling to North Macedonia from Serbia and Kosovo typically offer comfortable seating, dining options, and panoramic views of the countryside. International trains are equipped with modern amenities, including restrooms, Wi-Fi (where available), and onboard staff to assist passengers during their journey.

Border Crossings and Customs

When traveling by train into North Macedonia, passengers must pass through border crossings, where customs and immigration procedures are conducted. It's essential to carry valid travel documents, including passports and any necessary visas, and to comply with entry requirements imposed by North Macedonian authorities.

From Greece and Bulgaria

While direct train services from Greece and Bulgaria to North Macedonia are limited, travelers can reach North Macedonia via neighboring countries with robust rail networks. Routes through Thessaloniki in Greece and Sofia in Bulgaria offer connections to regional hubs, where travelers can transfer to buses or continue their journey by road into North Macedonia.

Planning Your Journey

For travelers considering train travel to North Macedonia, it's advisable to check schedules, ticket availability, and potential route changes in advance. International rail services may vary seasonally, so confirming details with railway operators or local travel agencies ensures a smooth and enjoyable journey through this enchanting Balkan destination.

Traveling to North Macedonia by train provides a scenic and culturally enriching experience, connecting visitors to the country's vibrant cities, stunning landscapes, and historical treasures. Whether embarking on a leisurely journey from Belgrade or exploring regional connections through neighboring countries, train travel offers an immersive way to discover North Macedonia's diverse attractions and hospitality.

CHAPTER FOUR

NAVIGATING NORTH MACEDONIA

Navigating North Macedonia offers travelers a chance to explore a blend of ancient history, natural beauty, and vibrant culture in the heart of the Balkans. Whether traveling by car, public transport, or on foot, understanding the country's transportation options and local customs ensures a smooth and enjoyable journey.

Transportation Options

Driving: Renting a car provides flexibility to explore North Macedonia's diverse regions, from bustling cities like Skopje to serene lakeside towns such as Ohrid. Major highways connect key destinations, although roads in rural areas may be narrower and winding. It's essential to familiarize yourself with local traffic laws and signage.

Public Transport: North Macedonia's public transport network includes buses and taxis, offering affordable and convenient travel between cities and towns. Bus services operate regular routes, with central stations in major cities like Skopje and Bitola. Taxis are readily available and can be hailed on the street or booked through hotel services.

Rail: While the country's rail network primarily serves regional connections, international travelers can access

North Macedonia by train from neighboring countries like Serbia and Kosovo. Trains offer scenic routes through mountainous landscapes, providing a unique perspective on the region.

Local Customs and Etiquette

Language: While Macedonian is the official language, English is widely spoken in tourist areas. Learning basic phrases in Macedonian, such as greetings and polite expressions, can enhance interactions with locals.

Hospitality: North Macedonians are known for their warm hospitality. When visiting homes or dining with locals, accept offers of food and drink graciously, and engage in polite conversation to show appreciation for their generosity.

Cultural Respect: Respect religious customs, particularly when visiting Orthodox churches and monasteries. Dress modestly and remove hats when entering religious sites to demonstrate respect for local traditions.

Practical Tips

Currency: The official currency is the Macedonian denar (MKD). Currency exchange services are available at banks and exchange offices.

Safety: North Macedonia is generally safe for travelers, but it's advisable to exercise standard precautions, especially in crowded or unfamiliar areas.

Emergency Contacts: Memorize or keep handy emergency numbers, including police (192), ambulance (194), and fire department (193).

Public Transportation

Navigating North Macedonia using public transportation offers travelers convenient and affordable options to explore the country's diverse landscapes, historical sites, and cultural attractions. Understanding the available modes of public transport ensures efficient travel between cities, towns, and rural areas.

Buses

Inter-City Buses: Buses are the primary mode of public transport for traveling between major cities and towns in North Macedonia. Skopje serves as a central hub, with regular bus services connecting to destinations such as Ohrid, Bitola, Tetovo, and Strumica. Buses are reliable, comfortable, and offer scenic views of the countryside.

Local Buses: Within cities like Skopje and Bitola, local bus networks provide convenient transportation for residents and visitors. Bus routes cover key areas within the city and suburbs, with frequent schedules during peak hours. Tickets can be purchased directly from the bus driver or at designated ticket booths.

Taxis

Taxis are readily available in urban centers and tourist areas throughout North Macedonia. They can be hailed on the street or booked through hotels and taxi companies.

Taxi fares are metered, and it's advisable to confirm the fare with the driver before starting the journey, especially for longer trips or airport transfers.

Trains

While North Macedonia's railway network primarily serves regional connections, trains provide an alternative mode of transportation for travelers arriving from neighboring countries like Serbia and Kosovo. The Belgrade-Skopje line offers a scenic route through mountainous terrain, with stops at key stations including Kumanovo and Veles.

Practical Tips

Ticketing: Purchase bus tickets from ticket booths or directly from the bus driver. In larger cities, electronic ticketing systems may be available.

Timetables: Check bus and train schedules in advance, especially for inter-city journeys, to plan your travel efficiently.

Language: While Macedonian is the official language, basic English is spoken in tourist areas. Having destination names and addresses written down in Macedonian can aid communication with drivers.

Car Rentals

Renting a car in North Macedonia provides travelers with flexibility and convenience to explore the country's diverse landscapes, historical sites, and scenic routes at their own pace. Understanding the process of renting a car ensures a smooth and enjoyable travel experience through this Balkan nation.

Rental Agencies

Major international car rental agencies such as Hertz, Avis, Europcar, and Budget operate in North Macedonia, with offices located at Skopje International Airport, Ohrid St. Paul the Apostle Airport, and in major cities like Skopje and Ohrid. Local rental companies also offer competitive rates and can be found throughout urban centers and tourist areas.

Requirements and Documentation

To rent a car in North Macedonia, travelers must typically meet the following requirements:

Age: The minimum age for renting a car is usually 21 years, although some agencies may require drivers to be 25 or older.

Driver's License: A valid driver's license from your home country is required. International driving permits (IDPs) are recommended for non-European Union license holders, although they may not always be mandatory.

Payment and Insurance: Credit card payment is generally required for car rentals, and insurance options (including collision damage waiver and theft protection) are available at the rental counter. Travelers should review insurance coverage options and policies before signing the rental agreement.

Booking and Reservation

It's advisable to book your rental car in advance, especially during peak tourist seasons or if you require a specific type of vehicle. Online booking platforms or directly through rental agency websites allow travelers to compare rates, select vehicle categories (such as economy, compact, SUV), and specify pickup and drop-off locations.

Driving in North Macedonia

Road Conditions: Major highways are well-maintained, but roads in rural areas may be narrower and winding. Exercise caution, especially during inclement weather.

Traffic Laws: Familiarize yourself with local traffic laws and regulations, including speed limits and parking restrictions. Seat belts are mandatory for all passengers.

Biking and Walking

Exploring North Macedonia on foot or by bicycle offers travelers an intimate and eco-friendly way to experience the country's diverse landscapes, cultural heritage, and local communities. Whether trekking through national parks or cycling along scenic routes, embracing these activities provides unique perspectives on this Balkan gem.

Biking

Scenic Routes: North Macedonia boasts picturesque biking trails, from the shores of Lake Ohrid to mountainous regions near Mavrovo National Park. Cycling enthusiasts can enjoy both leisurely rides and challenging routes that traverse varied terrain, offering stunning views of lakes, forests, and historic villages.

Bike Rentals: Several towns and tourist centers offer bike rental services, including Skopje, Ohrid, and Bitola. Rental options range from standard bicycles to mountain bikes and electric bikes, catering to different skill levels and preferences. It's advisable to book bikes in advance, especially during peak tourist seasons.

Cycling Etiquette: Respect local traffic laws and share the road with pedestrians and motor vehicles. Wear appropriate safety gear, including helmets, and carry sufficient water and supplies, especially on longer rides through rural areas.

Walking and Hiking

Nature Trails: North Macedonia features diverse hiking trails, from gentle paths around Lake Ohrid to challenging routes in Galicica National Park. Hikers can explore lush forests, ancient ruins, and panoramic viewpoints that offer glimpses of neighboring countries.

Trail Accessibility: Many hiking trails are accessible year-round, though conditions may vary with the seasons. Trails are generally well-marked, but it's advisable to obtain trail maps or seek local advice before embarking on longer hikes.

Cultural Heritage: Walking tours in cities like Skopje and Ohrid provide opportunities to explore historic landmarks, traditional markets, and architectural gems. Guided tours offer insights into North Macedonia's rich history and cultural traditions.

Practical Tips

Weather and Terrain: Check weather forecasts and trail conditions before setting out, especially in mountainous regions.

Respect Nature: Preserve the environment by staying on designated trails, disposing of waste responsibly, and respecting wildlife and local flora.

CHAPTER FIVE

ACCOMMODATION AND DINING

When visiting North Macedonia, travelers can expect a variety of accommodation options and a rich culinary tradition that reflects the country's cultural diversity and hospitality. From historic hotels to traditional guesthouses, and local taverns to fine dining restaurants, North Macedonia offers a range of choices to suit every taste and budget.

Accommodation Options

Hotels and Resorts: Major cities like Skopje and Ohrid feature international hotel chains offering modern amenities and comfortable stays. Boutique hotels in historical buildings offer a blend of charm and luxury, providing personalized service and unique cultural experiences. Additionally, resorts near Lake Ohrid and Galicica National Park cater to travelers seeking relaxation amid natural beauty.

Guesthouses and Bed & Breakfasts: Traditional guesthouses, locally known as "ethno houses," provide authentic Macedonian hospitality in picturesque settings. These accommodations often feature rustic decor, homemade meals, and personalized service, offering guests a glimpse into local customs and traditions.

Hostels and Budget Accommodations: Backpackers and budget-conscious travelers can find hostels and affordable guesthouses in major cities and tourist hubs. These accommodations offer basic amenities, communal spaces, and opportunities to connect with fellow travelers from around the world.

Dining Experiences

Traditional Cuisine: Macedonian cuisine blends Mediterranean and Balkan flavors, with dishes featuring fresh vegetables, grilled meats, and aromatic herbs. Local specialties include "Tavče gravče" (baked beans), "Ajvar" (roasted red pepper spread), and "Ohrid trout" (freshwater fish from Lake Ohrid).

Restaurants and Taverns: Cities like Skopje and Ohrid boast a vibrant dining scene with restaurants ranging from cozy taverns serving hearty meals to upscale venues offering gourmet cuisine. Waterfront restaurants in Ohrid provide stunning views of the lake, accompanied by fresh seafood dishes and local wines.

Street Food and Markets: Explore local markets in Skopje and Bitola for a taste of traditional street food such as "burek" (flaky pastry with fillings like cheese or meat) and "kebapčinja" (grilled sausages). These markets also offer fresh produce, homemade cheeses, and local sweets like "tulumba" (fried dough soaked in syrup).

Practical Tips
Reservations: During peak tourist seasons, especially in summer, it's advisable to book accommodations and restaurant reservations in advance.

Currency: The official currency is the Macedonian denar (MKD). Most establishments accept credit cards, but it's useful to carry cash for smaller purchases and markets.

Tipping: Tipping in restaurants is customary but not obligatory. A tip of around 10% of the bill is appreciated for good service.

Hotels and Resorts
North Macedonia offers a range of hotels and resorts catering to diverse traveler preferences, from historic landmarks to modern retreats amidst scenic landscapes. Whether seeking luxury accommodations or budget-friendly stays, visitors can find suitable options across the country's key destinations.

Skopje
Hotel Aleksandar Palace: Located in Skopje, this luxury hotel offers panoramic views of the city and Vodno Mountain. Address: Bul. Oktomvriska Revolucija br.15, 1000 Skopje, North Macedonia. The hotel features spacious rooms, a wellness center, and multiple dining options, making it ideal for both business and leisure travelers.

Hotel Arka: Situated in Skopje's Old Bazaar district, Hotel Arka combines traditional architecture with modern amenities. Address: Bitpazarska 90, 1000 Skopje, North Macedonia. Guests can enjoy proximity to historical sites and vibrant local markets, with comfortable rooms and a rooftop terrace offering views of the city skyline.

Ohrid

Hotel Belvedere: Overlooking Lake Ohrid, Hotel Belvedere offers a tranquil retreat near the town center. Address: Kej Makedonija bb, 6000 Ohrid, North Macedonia. The hotel features lake-view rooms, an outdoor pool, and direct access to a private beach, perfect for guests seeking relaxation and scenic beauty.

Villa St. Sofija: Located in the UNESCO-listed Old Town of Ohrid, Villa St. Sofija offers boutique accommodations in a historic setting. Address: Car Samoil 55, 6000 Ohrid, North Macedonia. Guests can explore nearby cultural landmarks and enjoy personalized service in this charming guesthouse.

Bitola

Hotel Epinal: Situated in Bitola's city center, Hotel Epinal combines modern comfort with proximity to local attractions. Address: 11 Oktomvri 1861 No.4, 7000 Bitola, North Macedonia. The hotel features elegant rooms, a spa center, and conference facilities, making it suitable for both leisure and business travelers.

Getting There

By Air: International visitors can fly into Skopje International Airport (SKP) or Ohrid St. Paul the Apostle Airport (OHD). From Skopje, hotels are accessible via taxi or airport shuttle services, with travel times varying depending on traffic.

By Car: Travelers arriving by car can access major cities and tourist destinations in North Macedonia via well-maintained highways and roads. GPS navigation and local maps are recommended for navigation within cities and to reach specific hotel addresses.

By Public Transport: Inter-city buses connect Skopje, Ohrid, Bitola, and other towns, with central bus stations providing access to local taxis or walking distance to nearby hotels.

Guesthouses

Guesthouses in North Macedonia offer travelers a unique opportunity to experience local hospitality, traditional charm, and personalized service in picturesque settings across the country. Whether nestled in historic towns or surrounded by scenic landscapes, these accommodations provide a welcoming atmosphere for visitors seeking an authentic Macedonian experience.

Skopje

Vila Silia: Located in the quiet neighborhood of Vodno, Vila Silia offers a peaceful retreat with easy access to

Skopje's city center. Address: Radoslav Shiskov Str. No.19, 1000 Skopje, North Macedonia. This guesthouse features comfortable rooms, a garden terrace, and homemade breakfast options, making it ideal for couples and solo travelers seeking tranquility.

Villa Vodno: Situated at the foot of Mount Vodno, Villa Vodno offers panoramic views of Skopje and convenient access to hiking trails. Address: Ljuben Lape Str. No.9, 1000 Skopje, North Macedonia. Guests can enjoy spacious accommodations, a shared kitchen, and a cozy lounge area, creating a home-away-from-home atmosphere.

Ohrid

Villa Kale: Located in the UNESCO-listed Old Town of Ohrid, Villa Kale offers rustic charm and proximity to cultural landmarks. Address: Car Samoil 1, 6000 Ohrid, North Macedonia. The guesthouse features traditional Macedonian architecture, courtyard gardens, and comfortable rooms with views of Lake Ohrid, perfect for history enthusiasts and nature lovers alike.

Villa Jordan: Overlooking Lake Ohrid, Villa Jordan provides a tranquil setting near the city center. Address: Kej Marsal Tito bb, 6000 Ohrid, North Macedonia. Guests can relax on the terrace, enjoy homemade meals, and explore nearby beaches and historic sites, making it an ideal choice for families and couples.

Bitola

Pansion Kostoski: Situated in Bitola's city center, Pansion Kostoski offers convenient access to local shops and restaurants. Address: Stiv Naumov 22, 7000 Bitola, North Macedonia. This guesthouse features cozy rooms, a shared kitchenette, and friendly staff who provide local tips and recommendations for exploring Bitola's attractions.

Getting There

By Air: International visitors can fly into Skopje International Airport (SKP) or Ohrid St. Paul the Apostle Airport (OHD). From Skopje or Ohrid airports, guesthouses are accessible via taxi services or airport shuttles, with travel times varying based on location and traffic conditions.

By Car: Travelers arriving by car can navigate to guesthouses in Skopje, Ohrid, and Bitola using GPS navigation or local maps. Parking facilities may vary by guesthouse, so it's advisable to inquire about parking options when booking accommodations.

By Public Transport: Inter-city buses connect Skopje, Ohrid, Bitola, and other towns, with central bus stations providing access to local taxis or within walking distance to nearby guesthouses.

Unique Stays

North Macedonia offers travelers an array of unique accommodations that highlight the country's cultural heritage, natural beauty, and distinctive charm. From traditional stone houses to eco-friendly lodges, these unique stays provide memorable experiences for visitors seeking authenticity and adventure in the Balkans.

Lake Ohrid Region

Villa & Winery Mal Sveti Kliment: Located in the village of Vevčani, this boutique guesthouse and winery overlooks Lake Ohrid and offers a tranquil retreat amidst vineyards and orchards. Address: Vevčani, 6337, North Macedonia. Guests can enjoy wine tastings, vineyard tours, and traditional Macedonian cuisine, making it an ideal destination for wine enthusiasts and nature lovers.

Mavrovo National Park

Hotel Radika: Nestled in the heart of Mavrovo National Park, Hotel Radika offers rustic elegance with panoramic views of Lake Mavrovo and the surrounding mountains. Address: Mavrovo, 1254, North Macedonia. The hotel features wooden chalets, a wellness center with thermal pools, and activities such as hiking, skiing, and wildlife watching, providing an immersive nature experience.

Matka Canyon

Hotel Canyon Matka: Situated near Matka Canyon, this eco-friendly hotel blends modern comfort with eco-conscious design. Address: Street 10 No. 17, Matka, North Macedonia. Guests can explore the canyon's caves, hike scenic trails, and enjoy boat rides on the Treska River, immersing themselves in Matka's natural wonders and tranquility.

Skopje Old Bazaar

Hotel Senigallia: Located within Skopje's historic Old Bazaar, Hotel Senigallia offers a blend of Ottoman architecture and contemporary luxury. Address: Bistrik 37, 1000 Skopje, North Macedonia. Guests can explore nearby bazaars, mosques, and museums, experiencing Skopje's cultural heritage while enjoying modern amenities and personalized service.

Getting There

By Air: International visitors can fly into Skopje International Airport (SKP) or Ohrid St. Paul the Apostle Airport (OHD). From these airports, unique stays are accessible via taxi services or rental cars, with travel times varying based on location and road conditions.

By Car: Travelers can reach unique accommodations in North Macedonia by navigating major highways and local roads. GPS navigation or local maps are recommended for finding addresses and navigating through cities and rural areas.

By Public Transport: Inter-city buses connect major towns and cities, with central bus stations providing access to local taxis or within walking distance to unique stays located in urban centers.

Online Booking Platforms

Online booking platforms provide convenient access to a wide range of accommodations, transportation options, and activities in North Macedonia, facilitating seamless travel planning for visitors exploring this Balkan destination. Whether seeking hotels, guesthouses, car rentals, or guided tours, these platforms offer comprehensive services to enhance the travel experience.

Accommodation Options

Hotels and Resorts: Major cities like Skopje, Ohrid, and Bitola feature a variety of hotels and resorts listed on online platforms such as Booking.com, Airbnb, and Expedia. Travelers can browse through a selection of accommodations ranging from luxury hotels with spa facilities to budget-friendly guesthouses in historic districts.

Guesthouses and Bed & Breakfasts: Traditional guesthouses and cozy bed & breakfasts in rural areas and cultural hubs are also available for booking. Platforms provide detailed descriptions, customer reviews, and photos to help travelers make informed decisions based on their preferences and budget.

Booking Process

Search and Compare: Start by entering your destination, travel dates, and preferences (e.g., budget, amenities). Online platforms offer filters to refine search results based on accommodation type, price range, and guest ratings.

Read Reviews: Customer reviews and ratings provide insights into the quality of accommodations and services. Travelers can read about experiences from previous guests to gauge the suitability of each option.

Booking Confirmation: Once you've selected an accommodation, proceed to book by entering your payment details and completing the reservation process. Confirmation emails with booking details and contact information are sent to your registered email address.

Transportation and Activities
Car Rentals: Online platforms also list rental car options from international agencies like Hertz and local providers, allowing travelers to compare prices, vehicle types, and rental conditions. Bookings can be made in advance, with options to pick up vehicles at major airports or city locations.

Guided Tours and Activities: Explore guided tours, cultural experiences, and outdoor activities offered in North Macedonia through online platforms. From city walking tours to hiking excursions in national parks, travelers can book activities that suit their interests and schedule.

Using Online Platforms
Accessibility: Access online booking platforms via desktop websites or mobile apps, offering user-friendly interfaces and multilingual support for international travelers.

Customer Support: Platforms provide customer support services, including live chat, email assistance, and 24/7 helplines, to address booking inquiries, modifications, or cancellations.

Payment Methods: Secure online payment systems accept major credit cards and offer options for payment in local currencies, ensuring transparency and convenience for travelers.

Online booking platforms play a crucial role in simplifying travel arrangements for visitors to North Macedonia, offering a diverse selection of accommodations, transportation services, and activities to suit every travel style and budget. Whether planning a city break in Skopje, a cultural tour in Ohrid, or an outdoor adventure in Mavrovo National Park, these platforms provide comprehensive tools and resources to enhance the travel experience and ensure a memorable stay in this enchanting Balkan nation. Embrace the convenience of online booking platforms to streamline your travel planning and discover the rich cultural heritage and natural beauty of North Macedonia with ease.

Regional Cuisine

North Macedonian cuisine reflects a rich tapestry of flavors influenced by Mediterranean, Balkan, and Ottoman culinary traditions. Known for its hearty dishes, fresh ingredients, and distinct regional variations, the country's cuisine offers a delightful exploration of local flavors and cultural heritage.

Traditional Dishes

Tavče Gravče: A national favorite, tavče gravče consists of baked beans seasoned with red pepper, onion, and garlic, often served as a side dish or a main course accompanied by freshly baked bread.

Ajvar: This roasted red pepper and eggplant spread is a staple in Macedonian cuisine, enjoyed as a condiment with bread or as a complement to grilled meats.

Ohrid Trout: Freshwater trout from Lake Ohrid is a culinary highlight, typically grilled and served with a side of salad or vegetables, showcasing the region's abundant natural resources.

Regional Variations

Skopje: The capital city offers a diverse array of dishes, including kebabs, stuffed peppers (filani piperki), and burek (flaky pastry filled with cheese or minced meat), influenced by Ottoman and Middle Eastern cuisines.

Ohrid: Located by Lake Ohrid, this region specializes in seafood dishes like grilled trout and Ohrid-style carp, paired with locally grown vegetables and aromatic herbs.

Pelagonia Region: Known for its agricultural produce, this region features dishes such as stuffed cabbage leaves (sarma), lamb stew (tepsija), and a variety of cheeses like sheep's milk cheese (sirenje) and white cheese (belo sirenje).

Dining Experience

Local Taverns (Kafani): Traditional taverns offer a cozy ambiance and serve homemade dishes like moussaka (musaka), bean soup (grashka chorba), and traditional desserts such as baklava and tulumba.

Market Cuisine: Street markets in cities like Skopje and Bitola feature stalls offering grilled meats, pastries, and sweets, providing a glimpse into everyday Macedonian culinary delights.

Traditional Dishes

North Macedonian cuisine is renowned for its rich flavors, hearty ingredients, and cultural significance, reflecting a blend of Mediterranean, Balkan, and Ottoman influences. These traditional dishes, cherished for their authenticity and regional variations, offer a delightful exploration into the country's culinary heritage.

Tavče Gravče

Tavče gravče, often considered the national dish of North Macedonia, features baked beans seasoned with red pepper, onion, and garlic. This hearty dish is typically served as a main course or side dish, accompanied by fresh bread and often enjoyed during festive gatherings and family meals.

Ajvar

Ajvar is a beloved condiment made from roasted red peppers, eggplant, garlic, and olive oil. It is popular throughout the Balkans and enjoyed in North Macedonia as a spread on bread, a topping for grilled meats, or as a flavorful addition to various dishes.

Shopska Salad

Shopska salad is a refreshing and colorful dish made with diced tomatoes, cucumbers, onions, and bell peppers, topped with grated white cheese (sirenje). Drizzled with olive oil and sprinkled with parsley, this salad showcases fresh produce and is a staple on Macedonian dining tables.

Sarma

Sarma consists of cabbage leaves stuffed with a savory mixture of minced meat (often pork or beef), rice, and spices. Slow-cooked in a tomato-based sauce, sarma is a comforting dish enjoyed during winter months and special occasions, symbolizing hospitality and family gatherings.

Desserts

North Macedonian desserts include baklava, a sweet pastry made with layers of filo dough, nuts, and honey; and tulumba, deep-fried dough soaked in syrup. These desserts, influenced by Ottoman cuisine, provide a sweet conclusion to meals and are often served during celebrations and festive occasions.

Dining Experience

Visitors to North Macedonia can experience these traditional dishes in local taverns (kafani), family-owned restaurants, and street markets throughout the country. These venues offer an authentic taste of Macedonian hospitality and culinary traditions, allowing travelers to immerse themselves in the country's rich cultural heritage through its flavorful cuisine.

Popular Restaurants

North Macedonia boasts a vibrant culinary scene with restaurants that showcase the country's rich gastronomic heritage, offering a blend of traditional flavors and contemporary dining experiences. From cozy taverns serving local specialties to upscale restaurants with panoramic views, here are some popular dining establishments worth exploring during your visit.

Skopje

Old City House Restaurant: Located in Skopje's Old Bazaar, this restaurant offers a charming ambiance with views of the Stone Bridge and Vardar River. Address: Kej Dimitar Vlahov 1, 1000 Skopje, North Macedonia. Guests can enjoy Macedonian and international cuisine, paired with local wines, making it an ideal spot for lunch or dinner after exploring nearby historical sites.

Restaurant Pelister: Situated near the City Park in Skopje, Restaurant Pelister specializes in grilled meats and traditional Macedonian dishes. Address: Bul. Partizanski Odredi 3, 1000 Skopje, North Macedonia. The restaurant's spacious terrace and elegant interior provide a relaxing setting for enjoying hearty meals and local specialties.

Ohrid

Kaj Kanevche: Located in the heart of Ohrid's Old Town, Kaj Kanevche offers a cozy atmosphere and panoramic views of Lake Ohrid. Address: Car Samoil 54, 6000 Ohrid, North Macedonia. Guests can savor fresh seafood dishes, grilled trout, and traditional Macedonian cuisine while taking in the picturesque surroundings.

Kaj Nikolče: Overlooking Lake Ohrid, Kaj Nikolče is renowned for its homemade Ohrid-style dishes and warm hospitality. Address: Kej Marsal Tito bb, 6000 Ohrid, North Macedonia. The restaurant's terrace provides a perfect setting for enjoying sunset views while indulging in local specialties and seafood delicacies.

Bitola

Tavče Gravče: Located in Bitola's city center, Tavče Gravče is a popular tavern known for its authentic Macedonian cuisine and casual atmosphere. Address: Marsal Tito 30, 7000 Bitola, North Macedonia. Guests can sample traditional dishes like tavče gravče, kebabs, and stuffed peppers, complemented by local wines and spirits.

Getting There

By Air: International visitors can fly into Skopje International Airport (SKP) or Ohrid St. Paul the Apostle

Airport (OHD). From these airports, restaurants in Skopje, Ohrid, and Bitola are accessible via taxi services or rental cars, with travel times varying based on location and traffic conditions.

By Car: Travelers can navigate to popular restaurants using GPS navigation or local maps. Parking facilities may vary by restaurant location, so it's advisable to inquire about parking options when planning your visit.

By Public Transport: Inter-city buses connect major towns and cities, with central bus stations providing access to local taxis or within walking distance to nearby restaurants located in urban centers.

Street Food and Markets

Exploring street food and markets in North Macedonia offers visitors a vibrant culinary adventure infused with local flavors and cultural richness. From bustling markets selling fresh produce to street vendors offering traditional snacks, here's a guide to experiencing the country's culinary delights:

Street Food Delights

Burek: A staple of Balkan cuisine, burek is a savory pastry filled with cheese, spinach, or meat, baked to perfection and often enjoyed as a quick snack or breakfast item.

Grilled Meats: Throughout North Macedonia, street vendors grill a variety of meats including kebabs (ćevapi), chicken skewers, and sausages (kobasica). These dishes are seasoned with local spices and herbs, offering a taste of traditional Macedonian flavors.

Ajvar and Pindjur: These flavorful spreads made from roasted red peppers, eggplant, and tomatoes are popular accompaniments to bread or grilled meats, showcasing the country's culinary diversity.

Local Markets

Skopje Central Market: Located near the city center at Majka Tereza 7, Skopje, North Macedonia, the Skopje Central Market is a bustling hub where locals gather to buy fresh fruits, vegetables, meats, and dairy products. The market also features stalls offering homemade jams, honey, and traditional Macedonian sweets.

Bit Pazar, Skopje: One of the oldest and largest markets in Skopje, Bit Pazar is renowned for its vibrant atmosphere and diverse array of products. Address: Bitpazarska bb, Skopje, North Macedonia. Visitors can explore stalls filled with fresh produce, spices, handmade crafts, and local delicacies, providing a sensory journey through Macedonian culture.

Ohrid Old Bazaar: In the heart of Ohrid's Old Town, the Ohrid Old Bazaar is a charming market where visitors can discover fresh fish from Lake Ohrid, local cheeses, and a variety of handmade goods. Address: Old Bazaar, Ohrid, North Macedonia. The market is a cultural hotspot offering an authentic taste of local life and traditions.

Getting There

By Air: International travelers can fly into Skopje International Airport (SKP) or Ohrid St. Paul the Apostle Airport (OHD). From these airports, visitors can reach markets in Skopje and Ohrid via taxi services or rental cars, with travel times varying based on location and traffic conditions.

By Car: Navigating to markets such as Skopje Central Market and Bit Pazar is convenient using GPS navigation or local maps. Parking options may vary, so it's advisable to inquire about parking facilities nearby.

By Public Transport: Inter-city buses connect major towns and cities, providing access to local markets within walking distance from central bus stations. Visitors can explore markets like Bit Pazar in Skopje and Ohrid Old Bazaar easily using public transport.

Food and Drink Etiquette

Understanding the nuances of food and drink etiquette in North Macedonia enhances the cultural experience for travelers.

Food and Drink Etiquette in North Macedonia

Hospitality and Respect: Macedonian dining customs emphasize hospitality and respect for guests. When invited to someone's home for a meal, it's customary to bring a small gift, such as flowers or chocolates, to show appreciation for the invitation. Upon arrival, wait to be directed to your seat and expect to be served hearty portions of food and drinks.

Communal Dining: Meals in North Macedonia are often communal affairs, with dishes served family-style. It's polite to try a bit of everything offered, even if just a small amount, to show appreciation for the host's efforts in preparing the meal. Complimenting the food is also customary and appreciated.

Starting and Ending Meals: Wait until everyone is served before beginning to eat. It's considered respectful to keep your hands visible above the table while dining. Additionally, pace yourself during the meal and engage in conversation with fellow diners to enjoy the communal aspect of Macedonian dining.

Tipping and Payment: In restaurants, tipping is appreciated but not mandatory. Rounding up the bill is generally sufficient. Payment is often made at the register after the meal, rather than at the table.

Drinks and Toasts: Macedonians enjoy toasting during meals, often with local wines or rakija (fruit brandy). When toasting, maintain eye contact and clink glasses with everyone present. It's polite to take a sip after each toast rather than emptying your glass in one go.

Conclusion: Understanding and respecting food and drink etiquette in North Macedonia not only enhances the dining experience but also fosters positive interactions with locals. By embracing these customs, travelers can fully appreciate the rich cultural heritage and warm hospitality that define Macedonian dining traditions.

CHAPTER SIX

REGIONS AND CITIES

North Macedonia, a land of diverse landscapes and rich cultural heritage, is divided into several distinct regions, each offering unique experiences and attractions.

Skopje Region

Skopje, the capital city, is the political, cultural, and economic heart of North Macedonia. Nestled in the Vardar River Valley, Skopje boasts a blend of ancient and modern architecture. Key attractions include the historic Old Bazaar, the iconic Stone Bridge, and the towering Millennium Cross on Mount Vodno. The city is also home to numerous museums, galleries, and vibrant nightlife.

Pelagonia Region

Bitola, the second-largest city, is known for its neoclassical architecture and historical significance. Located in the Pelagonia Valley, Bitola features the ancient city of Heraclea Lyncestis, with well-preserved Roman ruins. The city's famous Shirok Sokak Street is lined with cafes, shops, and charming buildings.

Prilep, another notable city in the Pelagonia region, is famous for its tobacco industry and medieval monasteries. The nearby Marko's Towers offer hiking opportunities and panoramic views of the region.

Vardar Region

The Vardar Region is named after the Vardar River, which flows through the heart of North Macedonia. Veles is an important industrial and cultural center, known for its historic churches and beautiful lakes. The city of Kavadarci is renowned for its vineyards and wineries, producing some of the best wines in the country.

Southwestern Region

Ohrid, often referred to as the "Jerusalem of the Balkans," is a UNESCO World Heritage site famous for its stunning lake and numerous churches. Ohrid Lake, one of Europe's oldest and deepest lakes, offers crystal-clear waters and a serene atmosphere. The city itself is rich in history, with ancient theaters, fortresses, and Byzantine churches.

Struga, located on the northern shore of Lake Ohrid, is known for its poetry festival and picturesque riverside setting. The town's unique position at the outflow of the Black Drim River into Lake Ohrid provides beautiful scenery and a tranquil environment.

Eastern Region

Štip is the largest city in eastern North Macedonia, known for its textile industry and vibrant cultural scene. The city hosts several festivals and boasts historical sites like the Isar Fortress and numerous churches.

Kočani, famous for its rice production, is surrounded by natural beauty, including the Osogovo Mountains and nearby thermal springs. The city offers a peaceful retreat with opportunities for hiking and exploring nature.

Skopje Region

The Skopje Region, encompassing the vibrant capital city of North Macedonia, is the country's political, cultural, and economic nucleus. Skopje, situated in the picturesque Vardar River Valley, offers a rich blend of historical heritage and contemporary development.

Skopje is a city of contrasts, where ancient landmarks coexist with modern structures. The city's historic core, the Old Bazaar, is one of the oldest and largest marketplaces in the Balkans. Wandering through its narrow, cobblestone streets, visitors can explore a variety of shops, traditional crafts, and Ottoman-era mosques, providing a glimpse into the region's rich past.

The iconic Stone Bridge, spanning the Vardar River, connects the old and new parts of the city. This historic bridge, dating back to the 6th century, is a symbol of Skopje and offers stunning views of the city's diverse architecture.

One of Skopje's most prominent landmarks is the Millennium Cross, perched atop Mount Vodno. Standing at 66 meters, it is one of the largest crosses in the world. Visitors can reach it by cable car, enjoying panoramic views of Skopje and the surrounding landscapes.

The city is also home to several museums and galleries that showcase its cultural and historical heritage. The Museum of the Macedonian Struggle, the Contemporary Art Museum, and the Archaeological Museum provide insightful exhibitions into the country's complex history and artistic achievements.

Skopje's vibrant nightlife and culinary scene reflect its diverse culture. The city offers an array of restaurants, cafes, and bars, where visitors can sample traditional Macedonian cuisine and international dishes.

Matka Canyon, located just outside Skopje, is a natural wonder offering outdoor enthusiasts opportunities for kayaking, hiking, and exploring ancient monasteries. The canyon's serene environment provides a perfect escape from the city's hustle and bustle.

Pelagonia Region

The Pelagonia Region, nestled in the southwestern part of North Macedonia, is renowned for its fertile plains, rich history, and cultural significance. This region encompasses several key cities and sites that offer a deep dive into the country's heritage and natural beauty.

Bitola, the second-largest city in North Macedonia, serves as a cultural and historical hub. Known for its neoclassical architecture, Bitola features the famous Shirok Sokak Street, lined with charming cafes, shops, and beautiful buildings. The city is also home to the ancient city of Heraclea Lyncestis, where visitors can explore well-preserved Roman and Byzantine ruins, including mosaics, a theater, and baths.

Prilep, another significant city in the Pelagonia region, is distinguished by its rich medieval history and scenic landscapes. The city is famous for its tobacco industry and numerous historical sites, such as the Marko's Towers. These medieval towers offer hiking opportunities and panoramic views of the surrounding area. Prilep is also known for its vibrant cultural scene, with festivals celebrating local traditions and arts.

The Pelagonia region is characterized by its agricultural productivity, particularly in the production of high-quality tobacco and wine. The region's vineyards and wineries, especially around the city of Kavadarci, are celebrated for producing some of the best wines in North Macedonia. Visitors can tour these vineyards, sample local wines, and learn about the winemaking process.

Kruševo, one of the highest towns in the Balkans, is a gem of the Pelagonia region. Known for its historical significance, Kruševo played a key role in the Ilinden Uprising against the Ottoman Empire. The town is also a hub for winter sports, offering skiing and snowboarding opportunities in the nearby mountains.

The Pelagonia Region is a captivating blend of historical richness, cultural vibrancy, and natural beauty. From the neoclassical charm of Bitola to the medieval allure of Prilep and the historical significance of Kruševo, this region offers a diverse and enriching experience for travelers. Exploring Pelagonia allows visitors to immerse themselves in North Macedonia's heritage, taste its renowned wines, and enjoy the stunning landscapes that define this remarkable region.

Vardar Region

The Vardar Region, located in central North Macedonia, is named after the Vardar River, which flows through its heart. This region is known for its agricultural productivity, historical sites, and vibrant cultural centers, making it a fascinating destination for travelers.

Veles, one of the principal cities in the Vardar Region, is an important industrial and cultural hub. The city is situated along the banks of the Vardar River, providing picturesque views and a serene atmosphere. Veles is renowned for its historic churches, such as the Church of St. Panteleimon and the Church of St. Nicholas, which showcase exquisite frescoes and traditional Macedonian architecture. The city is also home to the Poetry Night Festival, an annual event that celebrates literary arts and attracts poets from around the world.

Kavadarci, another significant city in the Vardar Region, is the heart of North Macedonia's wine country. Surrounded by vast vineyards, Kavadarci is famous for its wine production, particularly of the Vranec grape variety. Visitors can explore local wineries, such as the renowned Tikveš Winery, to sample and learn about the region's rich winemaking traditions. The annual Tikveš

Wine Festival is a highlight, offering wine tastings, traditional music, and cultural performances.

The Vardar Region is also home to Demir Kapija, a small town known for its stunning natural landscapes and outdoor activities. The Demir Kapija Gorge, with its dramatic cliffs and scenic vistas, is a popular destination for rock climbing, hiking, and bird watching. The area is part of the larger Vardar Valley, which is rich in biodiversity and offers numerous opportunities for nature enthusiasts.

Southwestern Region

The Southwestern Region of North Macedonia is a treasure trove of natural beauty, historical richness, and cultural heritage. This region, home to some of the country's most iconic landmarks and serene landscapes, offers a diverse array of attractions for travelers.

Ohrid, often referred to as the "Jerusalem of the Balkans," is the crown jewel of the Southwestern Region. This UNESCO World Heritage site is renowned for its stunning Lake Ohrid, one of the oldest and deepest lakes in Europe. The crystal-clear waters of the lake provide a picturesque backdrop for the town's historical sites, which include the Church of St. John at Kaneo, perched on a cliff overlooking the lake, and the ancient Theater of Ohrid, dating back to Hellenistic times. Ohrid's cobblestone streets are lined with traditional houses, shops, and cafes, offering a blend of history and modern charm.

Struga, located on the northern shore of Lake Ohrid, is another highlight of the region. Known for its annual Struga Poetry Evenings, an international poetry festival, Struga boasts a scenic riverside setting where the Black Drim River flows out of Lake Ohrid. The town's serene environment and beautiful landscapes make it a perfect spot for relaxation and cultural exploration.

The Southwestern Region is also home to the Galichica National Park, a vast area of mountains, forests, and diverse wildlife situated between Lake Ohrid and Lake Prespa. The park offers numerous hiking trails, breathtaking vistas, and opportunities for birdwatching, making it a haven for nature enthusiasts.

Bitola, the second-largest city in North Macedonia, is part of this region as well. Known for its neoclassical architecture and vibrant cultural scene, Bitola features the ancient site of Heraclea Lyncestis, with well-preserved Roman ruins that offer a glimpse into the region's historical significance.

Eastern Region

The Eastern Region of North Macedonia, often overlooked, is a hidden gem brimming with natural beauty, cultural heritage, and historical significance. This area offers travelers a unique glimpse into the country's diverse landscape and traditions.

Štip is the largest city in the Eastern Region and serves as a cultural and industrial hub. Known for its vibrant textile industry, Štip also boasts a rich history. The city is home to the Isar Fortress, a historic site offering panoramic views of Štip and its surroundings. Additionally, visitors can explore the Church of St. Nicholas, an architectural marvel with beautiful frescoes. Štip hosts several annual festivals, including the Štip Carnival and the Makfest Music Festival, showcasing local culture and talent.

Kočani, another prominent city in the Eastern Region, is famed for its rice production. The lush rice fields surrounding Kočani are a testament to the region's agricultural heritage. The city is also known for its geothermal springs, which offer relaxing and therapeutic experiences. Nearby, the Osogovo Mountains provide opportunities for hiking and nature exploration, with trails leading to scenic viewpoints and hidden monasteries.

Berovo, a small town nestled in the Maleshevo Mountains, is renowned for its serene natural beauty and clean air. Berovo Lake is a popular destination for fishing, boating, and picnicking, while the surrounding forests are perfect for hiking and wildlife spotting. The town is also famous for its traditional crafts, particularly wood carving and textile weaving.

Vinica is notable for the Vinica Fortress, an archaeological site with remnants dating back to the Roman and Byzantine eras. The town is also known for its pottery, and visitors can purchase beautifully crafted ceramics as souvenirs.

The Eastern Region of North Macedonia offers a rich tapestry of experiences, from historical exploration in Štip and Vinica to the natural tranquility of Kočani and Berovo. This region invites travelers to delve into its unique blend of cultural heritage and natural beauty, providing an enriching journey through one of North Macedonia's lesser-known yet captivating areas. Whether exploring ancient fortresses, enjoying local festivals, or hiking through mountainous landscapes, the Eastern Region promises a diverse and memorable adventure.

CHAPTER SEVEN

OUTDOOR ACTIVITIES

North Macedonia, a land of diverse landscapes and rich natural beauty, offers an array of outdoor activities for nature enthusiasts and adventure seekers alike. From rugged mountains and serene lakes to lush national parks and picturesque valleys, the country presents endless opportunities for exploration and enjoyment in the great outdoors.

Hiking and Trekking

North Macedonia is a paradise for hikers and trekkers, with numerous trails crisscrossing its varied terrain. The Osogovo Mountains in the Eastern Region are a haven for hiking, offering trails that lead to breathtaking viewpoints and historical monasteries. In the Southwestern Region, Pelister National Park near Bitola boasts the Baba Mountain Range, where hikers can explore dense forests and glacial lakes. Mount Vodno in the Skopje Region is another popular destination, featuring trails that provide panoramic views of the capital city and its surroundings. For those seeking a more challenging hike, Galichica National Park between Lake Ohrid and Lake Prespa offers diverse trails with stunning vistas of both lakes.

Water Activities

The lakes and rivers of North Macedonia provide a variety of water-based activities. Lake Ohrid, a UNESCO World Heritage site, is perfect for swimming, boating, and fishing. The crystal-clear waters of the lake attract visitors looking to enjoy water sports or simply relax on its shores. Berovo Lake in the Eastern Region offers a tranquil setting for fishing and boating, surrounded by the serene Maleshevo Mountains. Matka Canyon, near Skopje, is ideal for kayaking and exploring hidden caves, combining adventure with the natural beauty of the canyon's rugged landscape.

Skiing and Winter Sports

For winter sports enthusiasts, North Macedonia offers several excellent destinations. Mavrovo National Park in the Southwestern Region features the Mavrovo Ski Resort, which provides well-maintained slopes for skiing and snowboarding. The resort caters to all skill levels, making it a popular choice for families and seasoned skiers alike. The Osogovo Mountains also offer winter sports opportunities, with trails suitable for cross-country skiing and snowshoeing.

Rock Climbing and Mountaineering

The dramatic cliffs and rugged landscapes of North Macedonia make it a prime location for rock climbing and mountaineering. Demir Kapija Gorge in the Vardar Region is renowned for its challenging climbing routes and stunning views, attracting climbers from around the world. The Shar Mountain Range, straddling the border with Kosovo, offers some of the highest peaks in the country, providing exhilarating mountaineering experiences.

Cycling and Mountain Biking

Cycling enthusiasts will find a variety of trails and routes to explore in North Macedonia. The Vardar Valley offers scenic cycling paths through agricultural landscapes and picturesque villages. For mountain biking, the trails in Pelister National Park and the Osogovo Mountains provide challenging terrain and stunning natural scenery. The well-marked routes cater to both beginners and experienced riders, ensuring an enjoyable ride for all.

Wildlife and Bird Watching

North Macedonia's diverse ecosystems support a rich array of wildlife and bird species. Prespa Lake, shared with Greece and Albania, is a significant bird-watching destination, home to a variety of migratory and resident bird species. Mavrovo National Park and Galichica National Park also offer opportunities for wildlife spotting, including rare and endemic species. Guided tours and observation points are available for those looking to experience the country's rich biodiversity.

Hiking and Trekking

North Macedonia, with its diverse landscapes and rich natural beauty, offers a multitude of hiking and trekking opportunities across its various regions. Each region presents unique trails and scenic routes that cater to both novice hikers and seasoned trekkers.

Skopje Region

The Skopje Region, home to the nation's capital, boasts several notable hiking destinations. Mount Vodno, located just a short distance from Skopje (address: Vodno, Skopje 1000, North Macedonia), is a popular choice. Hikers can enjoy trails that range from moderate to challenging, culminating at the iconic Millennium Cross, which offers breathtaking views of the city and surrounding areas. The trailhead can be easily accessed from the city center, with public transportation options available.

Matka Canyon is another prime location, situated southwest of Skopje (address: Matka Canyon, Skopje 1000, North Macedonia). The canyon offers a network of trails that wind through rugged terrain, alongside the Matka Lake. Visitors can explore hidden caves, ancient monasteries, and enjoy panoramic views of the dramatic cliffs. The starting point of the trails can be reached by car or bus from Skopje.

Pelagonia Region

In the Pelagonia Region, Pelister National Park is a must-visit for hiking enthusiasts. Located near Bitola (address: Pelister National Park, Bitola 7000, North Macedonia), the park features the Baba Mountain Range. Trails such as the route to Pelister Peak (2601 meters) provide stunning views of glacial lakes, dense forests, and diverse flora and fauna. The park's visitor center in Bitola offers maps and information about various trails, making it an excellent starting point for treks.

Prespa Lake, straddling the borders of North Macedonia, Greece, and Albania, also offers scenic hiking opportunities. Trails around the lake provide serene landscapes, bird watching spots, and access to historical sites like the Monastery of St. Naum. Visitors can start their hike from the village of Stenje (address: Stenje, Resen 7317, North Macedonia).

Vardar Region
The Vardar Region, with its fertile valleys and agricultural landscapes, provides several picturesque hiking routes. Demir Kapija Gorge is a standout destination (address: Demir Kapija, 1442, North Macedonia). The gorge offers trails that lead through dramatic cliffs and along the Vardar River, ideal for both casual walks and more strenuous hikes. The town of Demir Kapija serves as a convenient base for exploring the area.

Tikvesh Region, known for its vineyards, also features hiking trails that combine natural beauty with cultural experiences. Trails around the town of Kavadarci (address: Kavadarci, 1430, North Macedonia) offer scenic views of vineyards, hills, and the Vardar River.

Southwestern Region
The Southwestern Region is home to some of the country's most iconic hiking destinations. Galichica National Park, located between Lake Ohrid and Lake Prespa (address: Galichica National Park, Ohrid 6000, North Macedonia), offers diverse trails with stunning

vistas of both lakes. Popular routes include the Magaro Peak Trail, which provides panoramic views of the surrounding landscapes. The park's visitor center in Ohrid offers detailed trail maps and guidance.

Mavrovo National Park is another gem in this region (address: Mavrovo National Park, Mavrovo 1254, North Macedonia). The park features trails that wind through dense forests, meadows, and along the shores of Mavrovo Lake. The hike to Korab Peak, the highest peak in North Macedonia, is a challenging but rewarding trek. The village of Mavrovo serves as a starting point for many of the park's trails.

Eastern Region
The Eastern Region, often overlooked, offers rich hiking experiences. The Osogovo Mountains are a highlight (address: Osogovo Mountains, Kriva Palanka 1330, North Macedonia). Trails lead to scenic viewpoints, historical monasteries, and diverse landscapes. The hike to Ruen Peak, the highest point in the Osogovo range, offers panoramic views of the surrounding areas. The town of Kriva Palanka provides access to many of the mountain's trails.

Berovo Lake, situated in the Maleshevo Mountains (address: Berovo Lake, Berovo 2330, North Macedonia), offers tranquil hiking trails around the lake and through pine forests. The trails are ideal for leisurely walks, picnics, and enjoying the serene natural environment.

The town of Berovo serves as a gateway to these hiking opportunities.

Skiing and Winter Sports

North Macedonia, with its diverse topography and mountainous regions, offers a variety of skiing and winter sports opportunities. Each region provides unique experiences, from well-developed ski resorts to pristine backcountry areas ideal for snowboarding, cross-country skiing, and other winter activities.

Skopje Region

The Skopje Region, while more urban, offers proximity to winter sports destinations. Mount Vodno (address: Vodno, Skopje 1000, North Macedonia) provides some opportunities for winter sports enthusiasts. Although primarily known for hiking and panoramic views, the slopes of Mount Vodno can be used for sledding and casual skiing during heavy snowfall. The cable car service, which operates year-round, offers access to higher altitudes where snow is more consistent in winter.

Pelagonia Region

The Pelagonia Region is home to Pelister National Park, near Bitola (address: Pelister National Park, Bitola 7000, North Macedonia). The park, known for its stunning natural beauty, transforms into a winter sports haven during the colder months. Pelister Ski Resort offers a variety of slopes catering to different skill levels. With well-maintained runs and facilities, it attracts both locals and tourists. Cross-country skiing is also popular in the park, with trails winding through snow-covered forests and around glacial lakes.

Vardar Region

While the Vardar Region is better known for its vineyards and agricultural landscapes, it offers some winter sports opportunities. The Kozuf Mountain (address: Kozuf Mountain, Gevgelija 1480, North Macedonia) features a ski resort that provides skiing and snowboarding facilities. The resort, still under development in parts, offers potential for winter sports enthusiasts looking for new terrains to explore. The surrounding areas provide picturesque views and opportunities for backcountry skiing and snowshoeing.

Southwestern Region

The Southwestern Region boasts some of North Macedonia's premier winter sports destinations. Mavrovo National Park (address: Mavrovo National Park, Mavrovo 1254, North Macedonia) is a key highlight. The Mavrovo Ski Resort, situated within the park, is the largest and most well-equipped ski resort in the country. It offers a variety of slopes for all skill levels, along with facilities for snowboarding, night skiing, and other winter sports. The resort's infrastructure includes ski lifts, rental shops, and accommodation options, making it a comprehensive winter destination.

Another notable area in this region is Galichica National Park (address: Galichica National Park, Ohrid 6000, North Macedonia). While primarily known for hiking and summer activities, the park's higher elevations receive substantial snowfall, allowing for backcountry skiing and snowshoeing. The park's stunning landscapes provide a scenic backdrop for winter adventures.

Eastern Region
The Eastern Region, often overlooked, offers significant winter sports potential. The Osogovo Mountains (address: Osogovo Mountains, Kriva Palanka 1330, North Macedonia) are a prime location. The Osogovo Ski Center, located near the town of Kriva Palanka, provides a range of slopes for skiing and snowboarding. The resort is well-regarded for its natural beauty and less crowded slopes, making it an attractive destination for winter sports enthusiasts seeking a quieter experience.

Additionally, the area around Berovo Lake (address: Berovo Lake, Berovo 2330, North Macedonia) in the Maleshevo Mountains transforms into a winter wonderland. The lake and surrounding forests offer opportunities for cross-country skiing and snowshoeing, with trails that traverse serene, snow-covered landscapes. The town of Berovo provides access and facilities for visitors.

Lake and River Activities
North Macedonia, blessed with numerous lakes and rivers, offers a plethora of water-based activities for visitors. From serene lakeside retreats to adventurous river escapades, each region provides unique opportunities to enjoy the country's aquatic treasures.

Skopje Region

The Skopje Region, while predominantly urban, is home to the picturesque Matka Canyon (address: Matka Canyon, Skopje 1000, North Macedonia). This stunning natural wonder offers a variety of water activities. Visitors can enjoy kayaking on the tranquil Matka Lake, exploring hidden caves like Vrelo Cave, and partaking in boat tours that showcase the canyon's rugged beauty. The canyon is easily accessible from Skopje, making it a popular day-trip destination for both locals and tourists.

Pelagonia Region

The Pelagonia Region features several lakes that offer diverse water activities. Prespa Lake (address: Prespa Lake, Resen 7310, North Macedonia) is a standout destination, straddling the borders of North Macedonia, Greece, and Albania. The lake is ideal for swimming, boating, and fishing, with serene waters and abundant birdlife creating a peaceful atmosphere. The village of Stenje provides access to the lake, with facilities for renting boats and organizing guided tours.

Pelister National Park near Bitola (address: Pelister National Park, Bitola 7000, North Macedonia) encompasses several glacial lakes, including Golemo Ezero. These high-altitude lakes are perfect for fishing and nature walks along their shores. The park's visitor center in Bitola offers information on accessing these scenic spots.

Vardar Region

In the Vardar Region, the Vardar River (address: Vardar River, Veles 1400, North Macedonia) plays a central role in the region's water activities. The river offers opportunities for kayaking, canoeing, and fishing. The town of Veles serves as a hub for organizing river excursions, with several local operators providing equipment and guided trips.

Tikvesh Lake (address: Tikvesh Lake, Kavadarci 1430, North Macedonia), situated near the town of Kavadarci, is another popular spot. The lake is known for its clear waters and scenic surroundings, making it ideal for boating, swimming, and fishing. Facilities for boat rentals and guided fishing tours are available in Kavadarci.

Southwestern Region

The Southwestern Region boasts some of North Macedonia's most renowned water destinations. Lake Ohrid (address: Lake Ohrid, Ohrid 6000, North Macedonia) is a UNESCO World Heritage site and a prime location for water activities. Visitors can enjoy swimming, sailing, kayaking, and diving in the lake's crystal-clear waters. The historic town of Ohrid offers numerous facilities, including boat rentals, diving schools, and guided tours that explore the lake's rich cultural heritage.

Lake Prespa, also in this region, provides a more tranquil alternative (address: Prespa Lake, Resen 7310, North

Macedonia). The lake is ideal for birdwatching, as it is home to many rare bird species. Visitors can enjoy kayaking, fishing, and peaceful boat rides, with access points in the villages of Oteševo and Stenje.

Eastern Region
The Eastern Region, characterized by its serene landscapes, offers several water-based activities. Berovo Lake (address: Berovo Lake, Berovo 2330, North Macedonia) in the Maleshevo Mountains is a serene spot perfect for fishing, boating, and picnicking. The lake's calm waters and surrounding pine forests create a tranquil setting, ideal for a relaxing day by the water. The town of Berovo provides access to the lake, with facilities for renting boats and organizing fishing trips.

The Bregalnica River (address: Bregalnica River, Štip 2000, North Macedonia) offers additional opportunities for water activities in the Eastern Region. The river is suitable for canoeing, kayaking, and fishing, with scenic routes that pass through lush landscapes and historical sites. The town of Štip serves as a gateway for exploring the Bregalnica River, offering equipment rentals and guided tours.

Boating and Kayaking
North Macedonia offers a rich array of opportunities for boating and kayaking enthusiasts. The country's diverse regions, each with its own unique landscapes and waterways, provide a range of experiences from tranquil lakes to adventurous river routes.

Skopje Region

In the Skopje Region, Matka Canyon (address: Matka Canyon, Skopje 1000, North Macedonia) is a prime destination for kayaking and boating. The serene Matka Lake, nestled within the canyon, is perfect for leisurely kayaking trips. Visitors can rent kayaks at the canyon's entrance and explore the calm waters, discovering hidden caves like Vrelo Cave and enjoying the picturesque scenery. Boat tours are also available, offering a guided experience through the stunning canyon.

Pelagonia Region

The Pelagonia Region is home to Prespa Lake (address: Prespa Lake, Resen 7310, North Macedonia), which offers excellent opportunities for boating and kayaking. The lake's expansive waters are ideal for exploring by boat or kayak, with several rental options available in the village of Stenje. Kayaking on Prespa Lake provides a unique perspective of its diverse birdlife and tranquil environment. Additionally, the smaller glacial lakes within Pelister National Park (address: Pelister National Park, Bitola 7000, North Macedonia) offer secluded spots for kayaking, surrounded by the park's natural beauty.

Vardar Region

In the Vardar Region, the Vardar River (address: Vardar River, Veles 1400, North Macedonia) is a popular choice for kayaking. The river's gentle flow in certain stretches makes it suitable for both novice and experienced kayakers. The town of Veles is a central hub for river activities, offering kayak rentals and guided tours.

Tikvesh Lake (address: Tikvesh Lake, Kavadarci 1430, North Macedonia), near Kavadarci, is another excellent location for boating. Its calm waters are ideal for a peaceful boating experience, with rental services available to facilitate a day on the water.

Southwestern Region

The Southwestern Region features the renowned Lake Ohrid (address: Lake Ohrid, Ohrid 6000, North Macedonia), a UNESCO World Heritage site. The lake's clear waters are perfect for kayaking and boating. Visitors can rent kayaks in the historic town of Ohrid and paddle along the lake's scenic shoreline, discovering hidden beaches and coves. Boat tours are also popular, providing an opportunity to explore the lake's cultural and natural landmarks.

Lake Prespa (address: Prespa Lake, Resen 7310, North Macedonia) in this region offers a more tranquil setting for kayaking. The lake, shared with Albania and Greece, provides peaceful waters ideal for a serene boating experience. Kayak rentals are available in the villages of Oteševo and Stenje, allowing visitors to explore the lake's diverse ecosystem and enjoy the surrounding mountain views.

Eastern Region

In the Eastern Region, Berovo Lake (address: Berovo Lake, Berovo 2330, North Macedonia) is a highlight for kayaking and boating. The lake's calm and clear waters, surrounded by lush pine forests, create an idyllic environment for a day of paddling. The town of Berovo offers kayak rentals and boating facilities, making it easy for visitors to enjoy the lake's tranquil beauty.

The Bregalnica River (address: Bregalnica River, Štip 2000, North Macedonia) also provides opportunities for kayaking. The river's scenic routes, passing through lush landscapes and historical sites, offer a mix of adventure and relaxation. The town of Štip serves as a base for river activities, with equipment rentals and guided tours available to explore the Bregalnica River's diverse waterways.

Fishing and Swimming
North Macedonia offers a variety of fishing and swimming opportunities across its diverse regions. From tranquil lakes to flowing rivers, each area provides unique settings for these water activities, ensuring a memorable experience for visitors.

Skopje Region
In the Skopje Region, Matka Canyon (address: Matka Canyon, Skopje 1000, North Macedonia) is a popular destination for both fishing and swimming. The calm waters of Matka Lake, surrounded by rugged cliffs, offer an ideal environment for swimming during the warmer months. Fishing enthusiasts can find spots along the lake and the Treska River, which flows through the canyon, to catch various freshwater species. The area provides a serene escape from the urban bustle, making it a favorite among locals and tourists alike.

Pelagonia Region

The Pelagonia Region is home to Prespa Lake (address: Prespa Lake, Resen 7310, North Macedonia), a prime location for fishing and swimming. The lake's clear waters are perfect for a refreshing swim, especially during the summer. Fishing is also popular, with ample opportunities to catch carp, trout, and other freshwater species. The village of Stenje offers access to the lake, with facilities for renting fishing gear and boats.

In addition, Pelister National Park (address: Pelister National Park, Bitola 7000, North Macedonia) features several glacial lakes, such as Golemo Ezero, where visitors can enjoy swimming and fishing in a more secluded and pristine environment. The park's visitor center in Bitola provides information on the best spots and necessary permits for fishing.

Vardar Region

In the Vardar Region, the Vardar River (address: Vardar River, Veles 1400, North Macedonia) is a prominent site for fishing. The river offers numerous spots along its course where anglers can fish for species like carp, catfish, and trout. The town of Veles serves as a central hub for organizing fishing trips and renting equipment.

Tikvesh Lake (address: Tikvesh Lake, Kavadarci 1430, North Macedonia), located near the town of Kavadarci, is another popular destination. The lake's warm waters are ideal for swimming, and its abundant fish population makes it a great spot for fishing. Facilities for boat rentals and fishing tours are available in Kavadarci, enhancing the overall experience for visitors.

Southwestern Region

The Southwestern Region boasts some of North Macedonia's most famous water bodies. Lake Ohrid (address: Lake Ohrid, Ohrid 6000, North Macedonia), a UNESCO World Heritage site, is renowned for its crystal-clear waters and rich biodiversity. The lake offers excellent conditions for swimming, with numerous beaches and designated swimming areas around the historic town of Ohrid. Fishing in Lake Ohrid is also a popular activity, with opportunities to catch unique species like the Ohrid trout and belvica. Fishing permits and gear rentals can be obtained in Ohrid.

Lake Prespa (address: Prespa Lake, Resen 7310, North Macedonia) provides a quieter alternative for swimming and fishing. The lake, shared with Greece and Albania, offers serene swimming spots and a diverse fish population. The villages of Oteševo and Stenje provide access points, along with facilities for fishing and swimming.

Eastern Region

In the Eastern Region, Berovo Lake (address: Berovo Lake, Berovo 2330, North Macedonia) is a top destination for both swimming and fishing. The lake's calm and clear waters, surrounded by pine forests, offer a picturesque setting for swimming. Fishing enthusiasts can enjoy the abundant fish population, including trout and carp. The town of Berovo provides access to the lake, with facilities for renting fishing gear and boats.

The Bregalnica River (address: Bregalnica River, Štip 2000, North Macedonia) also offers excellent fishing opportunities. The river's scenic routes provide numerous fishing spots where anglers can catch various freshwater species. The town of Štip serves as a base for river activities, offering equipment rentals and information on the best fishing spots.

Rock Climbing and Mountaineering

North Macedonia's diverse and rugged landscapes offer abundant opportunities for rock climbing and mountaineering enthusiasts. From dramatic canyons to towering peaks, each region provides unique challenges and breathtaking scenery.

Skopje Region

In the Skopje Region, Matka Canyon (address: Matka Canyon, Skopje 1000, North Macedonia) is a premier destination for rock climbing and mountaineering. The canyon features limestone cliffs with routes suitable for all levels of climbers, from beginners to advanced. Matka Canyon is well-equipped with marked trails and bolted climbing routes, ensuring safety and accessibility. Additionally, the nearby Vodno Mountain (address: Vodno Mountain, Skopje 1000, North Macedonia) offers hiking and mountaineering routes that lead to the iconic Millennium Cross, providing panoramic views of the city and surrounding landscapes.

Pelagonia Region

The Pelagonia Region, particularly within Pelister National Park (address: Pelister National Park, Bitola 7000, North Macedonia), offers exceptional mountaineering opportunities. Pelister Mountain, the highest peak in the park, stands at 2,601 meters and is a popular destination for mountaineers. The park's diverse terrain includes rocky peaks, glacial lakes, and dense forests, providing varied and challenging routes. Climbers can embark on guided tours or explore the marked trails independently. The park's visitor center in Bitola offers detailed maps and information on climbing routes.

Vardar Region

In the Vardar Region, the Kozuf Mountain Range (address: Kozuf Mountain, Gevgelija 1480, North Macedonia) is a prime spot for rock climbing and mountaineering. The range features rugged terrain with numerous climbing routes and hiking trails. Kozuf Mountain's peaks, reaching up to 2,171 meters, offer challenging ascents and stunning views of the surrounding valleys and plains. The nearby town of Gevgelija serves as a base for organizing climbing excursions and provides access to local guides and equipment rentals.

Southwestern Region

The Southwestern Region is renowned for its climbing and mountaineering sites, especially in Galicica National Park (address: Galicica National Park, Ohrid 6000, North

Macedonia). The park, situated between Lakes Ohrid and Prespa, offers a range of climbing routes on its limestone cliffs. The Magaro Peak, at 2,255 meters, is a popular mountaineering destination, providing sweeping views of both lakes and the surrounding mountains. The historic town of Ohrid is the gateway to the park and offers amenities and information for climbers.

Another notable site is Jablanica Mountain (address: Jablanica Mountain, Struga 6330, North Macedonia), located near the town of Struga. The mountain offers a mix of rock climbing routes and mountaineering trails, with its highest peak, Crn Vrv, standing at 2,257 meters. The area's natural beauty and varied terrain make it a favorite among outdoor enthusiasts.

Eastern Region
The Eastern Region boasts the Osogovo Mountains (address: Osogovo Mountains, Kriva Palanka 1330, North Macedonia), a prominent destination for rock climbing and mountaineering. The highest peak, Ruen, reaches 2,252 meters and offers challenging ascents for experienced climbers. The mountains are characterized by their rugged cliffs and diverse flora and fauna, providing a unique climbing experience. The town of Kriva Palanka is a convenient starting point for expeditions into the Osogovo Mountains, with local guides and equipment available.

Another highlight in the Eastern Region is the Kozjak Mountain (address: Kozjak Mountain, Kumanovo 1300,

North Macedonia). Known for its steep cliffs and rocky terrain, Kozjak offers a range of climbing routes for different skill levels. The mountain's proximity to the town of Kumanovo makes it easily accessible for day trips or extended climbing adventures.

Cycling and Mountain Biking

North Macedonia's diverse terrains and scenic landscapes make it a prime destination for cycling and mountain biking enthusiasts. Each region offers unique trails and routes, catering to both leisurely cyclists and adventurous mountain bikers.

Skopje Region

The Skopje Region provides a variety of cycling routes that cater to different skill levels. Vodno Mountain (address: Vodno Mountain, Skopje 1000, North Macedonia) is a popular spot for mountain biking. The trails on Vodno range from easy to challenging, with stunning views of Skopje and the surrounding countryside. For a more urban cycling experience, the Skopje City Park (address: City Park, Skopje 1000, North Macedonia) offers paved paths suitable for a leisurely ride, making it perfect for families and casual cyclists.

Pelagonia Region

In the Pelagonia Region, Pelister National Park (address: Pelister National Park, Bitola 7000, North Macedonia) stands out for its mountain biking opportunities. The park features numerous trails that wind through dense forests, along glacial lakes, and up rocky peaks. The Pelister

MTB Trail is particularly popular, offering a mix of technical sections and scenic views. The town of Bitola, with its charming architecture and vibrant culture, serves as an excellent base for cyclists exploring the park.

Vardar Region

The Vardar Region, with its vast plains and rolling hills, provides excellent routes for both road cycling and mountain biking. The Tikvesh Lake (address: Tikvesh Lake, Kavadarci 1430, North Macedonia) area offers picturesque routes through vineyards and along the lake's shores. The Kavadarci Cycling Trail is well-known among cyclists for its relatively gentle terrain and scenic beauty. The town of Kavadarci provides access to bike rentals and local guides, making it easy to plan a cycling trip in this region.

Southwestern Region

The Southwestern Region is a haven for cyclists, especially in Galicica National Park (address: Galicica National Park, Ohrid 6000, North Macedonia). The park offers a range of mountain biking trails with varying difficulty levels. The Galicica Ridge Trail provides challenging climbs and descents, with breathtaking views of Lake Ohrid and Lake Prespa. The town of Ohrid, a UNESCO World Heritage site, is a perfect starting point, offering bike rentals and detailed maps of the trails.

Another notable destination is Mavrovo National Park (address: Mavrovo National Park, Mavrovo 1256, North Macedonia). The park features numerous trails, including the popular Mavrovo Loop, which takes cyclists through diverse landscapes of forests, meadows, and around Mavrovo Lake. The village of Mavrovo offers amenities for cyclists, including accommodations and bike rental services.

Eastern Region
In the Eastern Region, the Osogovo Mountains (address: Osogovo Mountains, Kriva Palanka 1330, North Macedonia) provide excellent mountain biking opportunities. The area features rugged trails that challenge even experienced bikers. The Osogovo MTB Trail offers a mix of technical sections and stunning natural scenery. The town of Kriva Palanka serves as a gateway to the mountains, with local bike shops offering rentals and trail information.

The Bregalnica River (address: Bregalnica River, Štip 2000, North Macedonia) area is another attractive spot for cyclists. The Bregalnica Cycling Route follows the river, passing through picturesque villages and scenic landscapes. The town of Štip offers facilities for renting bikes and planning cycling tours along the river.

Wildlife and Bird Watching
North Macedonia boasts a rich biodiversity, offering exceptional opportunities for wildlife and bird watching. Each region, with its unique ecosystems and habitats, provides distinct experiences for nature enthusiasts.

Skopje Region

The Skopje Region, particularly Matka Canyon (address: Matka Canyon, Skopje 1000, North Macedonia), is a hotspot for bird watching. This scenic canyon is home to a variety of bird species, including the rare and endangered Egyptian vulture. Bird watchers can also spot peregrine falcons, golden eagles, and several types of owls. The lush vegetation and serene environment make Matka Canyon an excellent location for observing wildlife in their natural habitat.

Pelagonia Region

Pelister National Park (address: Pelister National Park, Bitola 7000, North Macedonia) in the Pelagonia Region is renowned for its diverse flora and fauna. The park is home to species such as the Balkan lynx, brown bear, and chamois. Bird watchers can look for the golden eagle, western capercaillie, and numerous species of woodpeckers. The park's varied landscapes, from dense forests to alpine meadows, provide ideal conditions for wildlife viewing. The visitor center in Bitola offers guided tours and detailed information on the park's wildlife.

Vardar Region

The Vardar Region, particularly around Tikvesh Lake (address: Tikvesh Lake, Kavadarci 1430, North Macedonia), is a prime area for bird watching. The lake and its surrounding wetlands are crucial habitats for numerous bird species, including the Dalmatian pelican, pygmy cormorant, and great white egret. The area is also home to various mammals such as wild boar and foxes. The town of Kavadarci provides facilities for organizing bird watching tours and offers information on the local wildlife.

Southwestern Region
Galicica National Park (address: Galicica National Park, Ohrid 6000, North Macedonia) in the Southwestern Region is a haven for bird watchers and wildlife enthusiasts. The park, located between Lakes Ohrid and Prespa, supports a wide variety of bird species, including the white-tailed eagle and the Eurasian eagle-owl. The diverse habitats of the park, ranging from oak forests to alpine pastures, also shelter mammals like the Balkan lynx and roe deer. The town of Ohrid is a convenient base for exploring the park, with guided tours available for wildlife observation.

Mavrovo National Park (address: Mavrovo National Park, Mavrovo 1256, North Macedonia) is another notable destination in this region. The park's extensive forests and high-altitude meadows provide habitats for species such as the brown bear, wolf, and wildcat. Bird watchers can expect to see the griffon vulture, black stork, and rock partridge. The village of Mavrovo offers amenities and guides for wildlife tours.

Eastern Region
The Eastern Region's Osogovo Mountains (address: Osogovo Mountains, Kriva Palanka 1330, North Macedonia) offer rich opportunities for bird watching

and wildlife observation. The mountains are home to the golden eagle, goshawk, and various species of owls. Mammals such as the European otter, wildcat, and red deer can also be found in the area. The town of Kriva Palanka serves as a gateway to the Osogovo Mountains, providing access to local guides and information on the region's wildlife.

The Bregalnica River area (address: Bregalnica River, Štip 2000, North Macedonia) is another significant spot for bird watching. The river and its wetlands attract species such as the common kingfisher, grey heron, and marsh harrier. The town of Štip offers facilities for organizing bird watching excursions and provides resources on the local avifauna.

CHAPTER EIGHT

NATURAL WONDERS

North Macedonia is endowed with a diverse array of natural wonders that are spread across its various regions. Each area offers unique landscapes, spectacular views, and rich biodiversity that make the country a fascinating destination for nature lovers.

Skopje Region

Matka Canyon (address: Matka Canyon, Skopje 1000, North Macedonia) is the Skopje Region's most notable natural attraction. Just outside the capital city, this stunning canyon is known for its steep limestone cliffs, tranquil Matka Lake, and an extensive network of caves, including the deep underwater Vrelo Cave. Visitors can enjoy activities such as kayaking, boat tours, and hiking on well-marked trails that offer breathtaking views and access to the area's rich biodiversity.

Pelagonia Region

In the Pelagonia Region, Pelister National Park (address: Pelister National Park, Bitola 7000, North Macedonia) stands out with its rugged terrain, lush forests, and glacial lakes. The park is famous for its unique Molika pine forests and the stunning views from the peaks of Mount Pelister. It is an ideal destination for hikers, offering trails like the Pelister Eye, which provides panoramic vistas of the surrounding landscapes and the city of Bitola.

Vardar Region

The Vardar Region is home to Demir Kapija Canyon (address: Demir Kapija, North Macedonia), a dramatic canyon known for its high limestone cliffs and scenic beauty. The Vardar River cuts through the canyon, making it a perfect spot for rafting and kayaking. The cliffs attract rock climbers from all over, and the area is also rich in birdlife, making it a great destination for bird watching. The town of Demir Kapija offers easy access and facilities for visitors.

Southwestern Region

Galicica National Park (address: Galicica National Park, Ohrid 6000, North Macedonia) is a prominent natural wonder in the Southwestern Region. Nestled between Lake Ohrid and Lake Prespa, the park boasts diverse ecosystems, including endemic flora and fauna. Trails like the Magaro Peak trail offer stunning views of both lakes and the surrounding mountains, making it a paradise for hikers and nature enthusiasts.

Lake Ohrid (address: Lake Ohrid, Ohrid 6000, North Macedonia), one of Europe's oldest and deepest lakes, is another gem of the Southwestern Region. Its crystal-clear waters and unique biodiversity have earned it a UNESCO World Heritage status. The lake is surrounded by historic towns such as Ohrid and Struga, and it offers a variety of water activities, including swimming, boating, and fishing.

Eastern Region

The Eastern Region is characterized by the scenic beauty of the Osogovo Mountains (address: Osogovo Mountains, Kriva Palanka 1330, North Macedonia). These mountains are home to dense forests, rich wildlife, and numerous hiking trails. The peaks offer panoramic views and are ideal for trekking and nature exploration. The town of Kriva Palanka serves as a gateway to these mountains, providing access and amenities for visitors.

Bregalnica River (address: Bregalnica River, Štip 2000, North Macedonia) is another natural wonder in this region. The river and its surrounding wetlands support a variety of bird species and provide opportunities for fishing and boating. The town of Štip offers facilities and guides for those looking to explore the river's natural beauty.

Matka Canyon

Matka Canyon, located just outside Skopje, is one of North Macedonia's most stunning natural attractions. Known for its steep limestone cliffs, emerald-green waters, and rich biodiversity, Matka Canyon offers a unique escape into nature.

Getting to Matka Canyon

Reaching Matka Canyon from Skopje is straightforward and convenient. The canyon is approximately 15 kilometers southwest of the city center, making it accessible by car, bus, or taxi. If driving, take the Makedonsko Kosovo Brigadi Boulevard out of the city, and follow the signs for Matka. The journey by car typically takes around 30 minutes. For those preferring public transportation, local buses from Skopje's main bus station (Autobuska Stanica Skopje) frequently run to the village of Matka. From the bus stop, it is a short walk to the canyon entrance.

Exploring Matka Canyon

Matka Canyon is renowned for its dramatic scenery and outdoor activities. Visitors can embark on hiking trails that wind through the canyon, offering breathtaking views and the chance to encounter diverse flora and fauna. The canyon is also home to several caves, including the renowned Vrelo Cave, one of the deepest underwater caves in the world. Guided boat tours are available, providing an opportunity to explore the caves and enjoy the tranquility of the Matka Lake.

Activities and Attractions

Kayaking on the calm waters of Matka Lake is a popular activity, offering a unique perspective of the canyon's towering cliffs. Equipment rental and guided tours are available at the entrance. The canyon also features medieval monasteries and churches, such as the Monastery of St. Andrew, which are accessible via hiking trails and boat tours.

Matka Canyon is a must-visit destination for nature enthusiasts and adventurers. Its proximity to Skopje makes it an ideal day trip for those looking to escape the city and immerse themselves in North Macedonia's natural beauty. With convenient access by car or public transportation, and a variety of activities to enjoy, Matka Canyon offers a memorable experience for all visitors.

Lake Ohrid

Lake Ohrid, one of Europe's oldest and deepest lakes, is a UNESCO World Heritage site renowned for its stunning natural beauty and unique biodiversity. Located in the southwestern part of North Macedonia, Lake Ohrid offers a tranquil escape with its crystal-clear waters and picturesque surroundings.

Getting to Lake Ohrid

Reaching Lake Ohrid is straightforward, whether you are coming from within North Macedonia or from neighboring countries. The nearest airport is Ohrid St. Paul the Apostle Airport (OHD), which is approximately 9 kilometers from the town of Ohrid. The airport receives seasonal international flights, making it a convenient option for international travelers. From the airport, a taxi or shuttle service can take you directly to the lake.

If you are traveling from Skopje, the capital city, the journey is approximately 170 kilometers and can be made by car or bus. By car, take the A2 motorway heading southwest, which offers scenic views and takes around 2.5 to 3 hours. Alternatively, regular bus services run from Skopje's main bus station to Ohrid, with a travel time of around 3.5 hours. The buses are comfortable and provide an affordable way to reach the lake.

Exploring Lake Ohrid

Lake Ohrid is celebrated for its pristine waters and rich history. The lakeshore is dotted with charming towns and villages, the most notable being Ohrid town, which boasts a wealth of historical sites, including ancient churches, monasteries, and a fortress. The town's cobblestone streets and traditional architecture provide a picturesque backdrop for leisurely strolls.

Activities and Attractions

Visitors can enjoy a variety of water activities such as swimming, boating, and fishing. Boat tours are available, offering scenic cruises around the lake and visits to nearby attractions like the Monastery of Saint Naum. The lake's unique ecosystem, which includes many endemic species, makes it a fascinating destination for nature enthusiasts and researchers.

Demir Kapija Canyon

Demir Kapija Canyon, located in the Vardar Region of North Macedonia, is a stunning natural wonder known for its dramatic limestone cliffs and scenic beauty. This canyon, which translates to "Iron Gate," is a paradise for outdoor enthusiasts and nature lovers, offering a range of activities amid breathtaking landscapes.

Getting to Demir Kapija Canyon

Reaching Demir Kapija Canyon is relatively straightforward, whether you're traveling from Skopje or other parts of North Macedonia. The canyon is situated about 100 kilometers south of Skopje, making it easily accessible by car or public transportation.

If you are driving from Skopje, take the E-75 highway south towards Gevgelija. The journey typically takes around an hour and a half. The highway is well-maintained and offers scenic views of the countryside. Once you reach the town of Demir Kapija, follow the signs leading to the canyon. The town provides ample parking facilities for visitors.

For those preferring public transportation, regular bus services operate between Skopje and Demir Kapija. Buses depart from Skopje's main bus station and the journey takes approximately two hours. Upon arrival in Demir Kapija, the canyon is a short walk or taxi ride away.

Exploring Demir Kapija Canyon
Demir Kapija Canyon is renowned for its impressive cliffs, which rise steeply from the Vardar River. The canyon is a popular spot for rock climbing, with numerous climbing routes catering to different skill levels. The cliffs' unique formations and challenging ascents attract climbers from around the world.

Activities and Attractions
In addition to rock climbing, the canyon offers excellent opportunities for hiking and bird watching. Trails wind through the area, providing stunning views of the canyon and its diverse flora and fauna. The Vardar River running

through the canyon is perfect for rafting and kayaking, offering thrilling adventures against a backdrop of natural beauty.

Osogovo Mountains

The Osogovo Mountains, located in the eastern part of North Macedonia, offer a majestic landscape characterized by rugged peaks, dense forests, and pristine wilderness. This mountain range is renowned for its natural beauty, rich biodiversity, and opportunities for outdoor activities.

Getting to Osogovo Mountains

The Osogovo Mountains are accessible from several entry points, depending on your starting location:

From Skopje

If traveling from Skopje, the capital city of North Macedonia, the Osogovo Mountains are approximately 70 kilometers northeast. The journey by car typically takes around 1.5 to 2 hours, depending on the route taken. Follow the E-871 highway east towards Kumanovo, and then continue towards Kriva Palanka. From Kriva Palanka, follow the signs leading into the mountains. The roads are well-maintained but can be winding as they ascend into higher elevations.

Public transportation options include buses from Skopje to Kriva Palanka, from where you can arrange local transportation or hike into the mountains. Buses depart regularly from Skopje's main bus station.

From Kriva Palanka

Kriva Palanka serves as a gateway to the Osogovo Mountains, offering access to hiking trails and mountain roads leading deeper into the range. Local transportation, such as taxis or hired vehicles, can take you to specific trailheads or scenic viewpoints within the mountains.

Exploring Osogovo Mountains

Osogovo Mountains are a haven for outdoor enthusiasts, offering activities such as hiking, trekking, and mountaineering. The region boasts a network of trails that cater to various skill levels, from leisurely walks through alpine meadows to challenging ascents of rugged peaks. Popular trails include routes to the highest peak, Ruen (2251 meters), which rewards hikers with panoramic views of the surrounding valleys and peaks.

Attractions and Natural Beauty
Apart from hiking, Osogovo Mountains are known for their diverse flora and fauna, including rare species of plants and animals endemic to the region. The mountain slopes are covered with forests of beech, oak, and coniferous trees, creating a picturesque backdrop for outdoor activities year-round.

Osogovo Mountains offer a serene retreat into nature, where visitors can immerse themselves in the pristine landscapes and diverse ecosystems of eastern North

Macedonia. Whether embarking on a challenging hike to a mountain summit or simply enjoying the tranquility of the wilderness, Osogovo Mountains provide an enriching experience for adventurers and nature lovers alike.

Bregalnica River

The Bregalnica River, flowing through the eastern part of North Macedonia, is the country's second longest river and a vital waterway for the region. Known for its picturesque landscapes and serene environment, the Bregalnica River offers a variety of outdoor activities and natural beauty, making it an ideal destination for nature enthusiasts and adventurers alike.

Getting to Bregalnica River

From Skopje

Travelers from Skopje, the capital of North Macedonia, can reach the Bregalnica River by car or public transportation. The river is approximately 100 kilometers southeast of Skopje. By car, take the A1/E75 motorway heading south, then merge onto the A4 towards Štip. The journey typically takes around 1.5 to 2 hours, depending on traffic conditions. Štip, one of the major cities along the Bregalnica River, serves as an excellent starting point for exploring the river and its surroundings.

For those preferring public transportation, regular bus services operate from Skopje to Štip. Buses depart from the main bus station in Skopje, and the journey usually takes around 2 hours. Once in Štip, local transportation options, including taxis and buses, can take you closer to the river and various points of interest along its course.

Exploring Bregalnica River

The Bregalnica River meanders through diverse landscapes, including lush forests, rolling hills, and fertile plains. It provides ample opportunities for recreational activities such as fishing, kayaking, and bird watching. The river's banks are lined with charming villages and historical sites, offering a glimpse into the region's rich cultural heritage.

One notable spot along the Bregalnica River is the town of Berovo, known for its scenic beauty and tranquil atmosphere. Berovo Lake, formed by the Bregalnica River, is a popular destination for swimming, picnicking, and hiking. The town of Vinica, another significant location along the river, is renowned for its medieval fortress and unique terracotta icons.

Natural Beauty and Attractions

The Bregalnica River basin is home to diverse flora and fauna, making it a haven for nature lovers. The area is rich in biodiversity, with numerous plant and animal species thriving in the river's ecosystem. The river's clean, clear waters and the surrounding natural landscapes create an idyllic setting for outdoor adventures and relaxation.

CHAPTER NINE

MUSEUMS, PARKS AND GARDEN

North Macedonia, rich in history and natural beauty, boasts a plethora of museums, parks, and gardens across its regions. Each location offers unique insights into the country's cultural heritage and natural splendor. Below is a comprehensive guide to these attractions, focusing on how to get there.

Skopje Region
Museums
Museum of the Macedonian Struggle: Located in Skopje, this museum presents the country's struggle for independence. It is situated on Ilindenska Street. From Skopje's city center, it is a short walk or a brief taxi ride. Museum of Contemporary Art: Perched on the hill of Kale Fortress, it showcases modern Macedonian art. Accessible via taxi or by a 15-minute walk from the city center.

Parks and Gardens
City Park (Gradski Park): A vast urban park in Skopje, offering walking paths, lakes, and playgrounds. It is centrally located, making it easily accessible on foot or by local bus routes.
Matka Canyon: A short drive from Skopje, Matka Canyon offers stunning natural scenery and recreational

activities. It is about 15 kilometers southwest of Skopje, accessible by car or bus.

Pelagonia Region

Museums

Bitola Museum: Located in Bitola, this museum houses archaeological and ethnographic exhibits. It is situated in the center of Bitola, easily reachable by foot or a short taxi ride.

Heraclea Lyncestis: An ancient city near Bitola with impressive mosaics and ruins. It is a 10-minute drive from Bitola's center.

Parks and Gardens

Pelister National Park: Near Bitola, this park is known for its rich biodiversity and hiking trails. About 14 kilometers from Bitola, it can be reached by car or organized tours.

Mogila Park: A peaceful park in the heart of Bitola, perfect for relaxing walks. Centrally located and easily accessible by foot or local transport.

Vardar Region

Museums

Veles Museum: Located in Veles, this museum focuses on regional history and culture. Situated in the city center, it is accessible by foot or local transportation.

Museum of Gevgelija: Showcasing archaeological finds and regional history, this museum is centrally located in Gevgelija.

Parks and Gardens
Lake Mladost: Near Veles, this lake is a popular spot for picnics and water activities. It is about 5 kilometers from Veles, reachable by car or taxi.
City Park Gevgelija: A well-maintained park in Gevgelija, ideal for family outings. Centrally located and accessible by foot.

Southwestern Region
Museums
Ohrid Museum: Located in Ohrid, this museum features a rich collection of historical artifacts. Situated in the city center, it is easily accessible on foot.

Struga Museum: Showcasing ethnographic and historical exhibits, this museum is located in Struga's center.

Parks and Gardens
Galicica National Park: Between Lake Ohrid and Lake Prespa, this park offers stunning landscapes and diverse flora and fauna. Accessible by car from Ohrid or Struga.

Ohrid Lake Promenade: A scenic walkway along Lake Ohrid, perfect for leisurely strolls. Centrally located in Ohrid and accessible by foot.

Eastern Region

Museums

Museum of Vinica: This museum in Vinica showcases terracotta icons and regional artifacts. It is centrally located in Vinica, easily reachable by foot or taxi.

Kochani Museum: Featuring exhibits on local history and culture, this museum is located in the center of Kochani.

Parks and Gardens

Berovo Lake: Near Berovo, this lake offers beautiful scenery and outdoor activities. It is about 7 kilometers from Berovo, accessible by car or taxi.

City Park Stip: A peaceful park in the heart of Stip, ideal for relaxation. Centrally located and accessible by foot.

Museum of the Macedonian Struggle

The Museum of the Macedonian Struggle, located at Ilindenska Street, Skopje, is a significant landmark dedicated to the country's pursuit of independence and national identity. This museum, established to honor and preserve the memory of the various revolts and movements that led to Macedonian sovereignty, provides an immersive historical experience through its extensive collection of artifacts, documents, and multimedia displays.

Exhibits and Highlights

Visitors to the museum can expect a well-curated chronological journey through Macedonia's tumultuous history. The exhibits highlight critical events, from the early uprisings against Ottoman rule to the more recent struggles for independence. Key artifacts include personal belongings of revolutionary leaders, rare photographs, and detailed maps that illustrate the geopolitical changes over the centuries. Interactive displays and multimedia presentations further enrich the visitor experience, making history accessible and engaging.

Getting There

The Museum of the Macedonian Struggle is centrally located in Skopje, making it easily accessible from various parts of the city. If you are in the city center, the museum is within walking distance, approximately a 10-minute stroll from Macedonia Square. For those using public transportation, numerous bus routes stop nearby. Taxis are also a convenient option and can drop you off directly at the museum's entrance. The precise address is Ilindenska Street, Skopje, North Macedonia.

This museum is a must-visit for anyone interested in understanding the depth and breadth of Macedonian history, providing valuable insights into the nation's enduring quest for freedom and identity.

Museum of Contemporary Art

The Museum of Contemporary Art in Skopje, North Macedonia, stands as a beacon of modern artistic expression, showcasing the dynamic and evolving landscape of contemporary art. Established in the aftermath of the 1963 earthquake, the museum was a symbol of global solidarity, as contributions came from artists worldwide to help rebuild the cultural heritage of the city.

Exhibits and Highlights

The museum boasts an impressive collection of over 5,000 works, including paintings, sculptures, and multimedia installations from both Macedonian and international artists. The exhibits are designed to challenge conventional perspectives, offering a platform for avant-garde and experimental works. Key highlights include pieces by renowned artists such as Pablo Picasso, Alexander Calder, and Joan Miró, alongside notable Macedonian artists like Petar Mazev and Nikola Martinoski. Temporary exhibitions and events further enrich the museum's offerings, providing fresh insights and new dimensions to contemporary art.

Getting There

The Museum of Contemporary Art is situated on the hill of Kale Fortress, offering not only artistic but also panoramic visual experiences of Skopje. The address is Samoilova bb, Skopje, North Macedonia. To reach the museum, visitors can take a taxi from the city center, which is approximately a 10-minute ride. Alternatively, public buses running through the central routes can get you close to the Kale Fortress, from where a short uphill walk will lead you to the museum. For those who prefer walking, it is about a 20-minute walk from Macedonia Square, through some of the city's scenic routes.

The Museum of Contemporary Art provides a unique and enriching experience, making it a must-visit destination for art enthusiasts and those interested in the cultural fabric of North Macedonia.

City Park (Gradski Park)

City Park, locally known as Gradski Park, is a sprawling urban oasis in the heart of Skopje, North Macedonia. This expansive park is a favorite among locals and visitors alike, offering a tranquil retreat from the city's hustle and bustle.

Features and Highlights

Spanning over several hectares, City Park is characterized by its lush greenery, beautiful flower beds, and serene lakes. The park features walking and cycling paths, playgrounds, and sports facilities, making it an ideal spot for recreation and relaxation. Notable attractions within the park include the Skopje Zoo, the City Stadium, and a variety of cafes and restaurants where visitors can enjoy refreshments while taking in the scenic views. The park also hosts various cultural events, concerts, and festivals throughout the year, adding to its vibrant atmosphere.

Getting There

City Park is conveniently located near the city center of Skopje, making it easily accessible by various modes of transportation. The park's address is Nikola Vapcarov bb, Skopje, North Macedonia. If you are staying in the city center, the park is within walking distance, approximately a 15-minute walk from Macedonia Square. For those using public transportation, several bus lines stop near the park's entrances. Taxis are also readily available and can drop you off at any of the park's multiple entrances.

Whether you are looking for a place to unwind, enjoy a leisurely walk, or participate in outdoor activities, City Park offers a refreshing escape in the midst of Skopje's urban landscape.

Bitola Museum

The Bitola Museum, located in the historic town of Bitola, North Macedonia, is a repository of the region's rich cultural heritage and history. Housed in the former military academy where Mustafa Kemal Atatürk, the founder of modern Turkey, once studied, the museum offers a fascinating glimpse into the area's past.

Exhibits and Highlights

The museum's diverse collection spans several periods, from ancient times to the modern era. Key exhibits include archaeological artifacts from the ancient city of Heraclea Lyncestis, ethnographic displays showcasing traditional Macedonian culture, and an extensive section dedicated to Atatürk's time in Bitola. The museum also features art galleries, historical documents, and multimedia presentations that provide deeper insights into the local history and heritage. Special exhibitions and cultural events are regularly held, adding dynamic elements to the museum's offerings.

Getting There

The Bitola Museum is centrally located at Shirok Sokak Street, Bitola, North Macedonia. Visitors coming from Skopje can take a direct bus or train to Bitola, which is approximately a two-hour journey. From the Bitola bus or train station, the museum is a short taxi ride away. For those exploring the town on foot, the museum is easily accessible from the main square, a pleasant 10-minute walk through the picturesque Shirok Sokak Street, known for its vibrant atmosphere and historic architecture.

This museum is a must-visit for history enthusiasts and those interested in the cultural evolution of North Macedonia, offering a comprehensive and engaging experience in one of the country's most storied towns.

Heraclea Lyncestis

Heraclea Lyncestis, an ancient city founded by Philip II of Macedon in the 4th century BC, is one of North Macedonia's most significant archaeological sites. Located near the modern town of Bitola, this historical treasure offers a captivating glimpse into the ancient world.

Historical Significance and Highlights

Heraclea Lyncestis thrived during the Hellenistic, Roman, and early Byzantine periods. Visitors can explore well-preserved ruins, including the Roman baths, basilicas, and the ancient theater, which is still used for performances today. The site is renowned for its stunning mosaics, particularly those in the Great Basilica, depicting intricate designs and vibrant scenes from early Christian iconography. In addition to architectural remains, numerous artifacts uncovered at Heraclea are displayed in the nearby Bitola Museum, providing further context to the site's historical narrative.

Getting There

Heraclea Lyncestis is located approximately 2 kilometers south of Bitola. The exact address is Heraclea Lyncestis, Bitola 7000, North Macedonia. Visitors traveling from Skopje can take a bus or train to Bitola, which is around a two-hour journey. Upon arriving in Bitola, the archaeological site is easily accessible by taxi or a brief car ride. For those preferring to walk, the site can be reached by a pleasant 30-minute stroll from the town center, passing through Bitola's charming streets and scenic views.

Exploring Heraclea Lyncestis provides an enriching experience, allowing visitors to step back in time and witness the grandeur of ancient Macedonian civilization amidst the serene landscapes of North Macedonia.

Pelister National Park

Pelister National Park, established in 1948, is one of North Macedonia's oldest and most stunning natural reserves. Located in the southwestern part of the country, near the town of Bitola, the park is renowned for its pristine landscapes, diverse flora and fauna, and the majestic Baba Mountain.

Natural Beauty and Highlights

The park covers an area of over 171 square kilometers, offering visitors a chance to explore its dense forests, clear streams, and picturesque lakes. One of the park's most famous features is the Molika pine, a rare species found only in the Balkans. Outdoor enthusiasts can enjoy various activities such as hiking, mountaineering, and bird watching. The park's trails, ranging from easy walks to challenging treks, lead to breathtaking viewpoints and natural wonders, including the Great Lake (Golemo Ezero) and the Small Lake (Malo Ezero). During winter, Pelister transforms into a haven for winter sports, particularly skiing and snowboarding.

Getting There

Pelister National Park is situated near the town of Bitola, making it easily accessible for visitors. The park's main entrance is located at the village of Malovishte. The address for navigation is Pelister National Park, Bitola

7000, North Macedonia. Travelers from Skopje can take a bus or train to Bitola, which is approximately a two-hour journey. From Bitola, the park is a short 20-minute drive by car or taxi. For those who prefer public transportation, local buses and minibuses also provide connections to the park's entrance.

A visit to Pelister National Park offers a refreshing escape into nature, where the serene environment and diverse wildlife provide an unforgettable experience in the heart of North Macedonia.

Mogila Park

Mogila Park, located in the town of Bitola, North Macedonia, is a serene and historically significant green space that serves as a memorial to the fallen soldiers of World War I. This beautifully landscaped park offers visitors a tranquil environment to relax and reflect amidst lush greenery and historical monuments.

Historical Significance and Highlights

Mogila Park, also known as the Memorial Park of the Revolution, is dedicated to the soldiers who lost their lives during World War I. The centerpiece of the park is the impressive Mogila Monument, a towering structure that honors the memory of these soldiers. The park is adorned with well-maintained gardens, walking paths, and benches, making it an ideal spot for leisurely strolls and quiet contemplation. Additionally, the park hosts various cultural events and activities throughout the year, further enriching its significance to the local community and visitors alike.

Getting There

Mogila Park is conveniently located in the town of Bitola, making it easily accessible for both locals and tourists. The address for navigation is Mogila Park, Bitola 7000, North Macedonia. Travelers coming from Skopje can reach Bitola by bus or train, a journey that typically takes around two hours. Once in Bitola, the park is situated close to the town center, making it reachable on foot within 10-15 minutes. Alternatively, local taxis are readily available for a short drive to the park's entrance.

Visiting Mogila Park provides a peaceful escape and a chance to pay respects to the historical legacy of the region, all within a beautifully landscaped setting that highlights the natural charm of Bitola.

Veles Museum

The Veles Museum, located in the heart of Veles, North Macedonia, offers a fascinating glimpse into the region's rich history and cultural heritage. Established in 1947, the museum is renowned for its extensive collection of artifacts, art, and historical exhibits that span several centuries.

Exhibits and Highlights

The museum's collection includes archaeological finds from the ancient Paeonian and Roman periods, showcasing the early history of the area. Visitors can also explore exhibits featuring medieval artifacts, ethnographic displays, and an impressive array of fine arts. The museum houses significant works from prominent Macedonian artists, providing insights into the country's artistic evolution. One of the museum's highlights is its comprehensive collection of items related to the Ilinden Uprising and the Macedonian struggle for independence, offering a deep dive into the national history and identity.

Getting There

Veles Museum is conveniently situated in the town center, making it easily accessible to visitors. The address for navigation is 11 Oktomvri 1, Veles 1400, North Macedonia. For those traveling from Skopje, the capital city, Veles is approximately a 45-minute drive via the A1 motorway. Regular bus and train services connect Skopje to Veles, making public transport a viable option. Upon arriving in Veles, the museum is within walking distance from the main bus and train stations. Local taxis are also available for a quick and convenient ride to the museum's entrance.

A visit to the Veles Museum offers a rich cultural experience, immersing visitors in the diverse historical tapestry of North Macedonia while enjoying the town's charming atmosphere.

Museum of Gevgelija

The Museum of Gevgelija, situated in the town of Gevgelija in North Macedonia, provides an enriching experience for visitors keen on exploring the region's historical and cultural legacy. The museum boasts an impressive collection of artifacts and exhibits that narrate the rich tapestry of Gevgelija's past, from ancient times through to the modern era.

Exhibits and Highlights

The museum's collection features archaeological artifacts from the prehistoric, ancient, and medieval periods, including pottery, tools, and decorative items that shed light on the early civilizations that inhabited the region. Additionally, the museum showcases ethnographic displays highlighting traditional Macedonian customs, clothing, and daily life, offering a glimpse into the cultural heritage of Gevgelija. The museum also hosts temporary exhibitions and cultural events, adding a dynamic element to its permanent collection.

Getting There

The Museum of Gevgelija is conveniently located at Marshall Tito 1, Gevgelija 1480, North Macedonia. For visitors traveling from Skopje, the capital city, Gevgelija is approximately a 90-minute drive via the A1 motorway. Regular bus and train services connect Skopje to Gevgelija, making public transport a convenient option. Upon arriving in Gevgelija, the museum is centrally located and easily accessible on foot from the main bus and train stations. Local taxis are also available for a short ride to the museum's entrance.

A visit to the Museum of Gevgelija offers an engaging journey through the region's history and culture, making it a must-see attraction for anyone exploring North Macedonia.

Lake Mladost

Lake Mladost, a picturesque reservoir located near Veles, North Macedonia, is a popular destination for both locals and tourists seeking relaxation and outdoor activities. Surrounded by serene landscapes and offering a range of recreational opportunities, Lake Mladost is an ideal spot for nature enthusiasts.

Attractions and Activities

The lake's tranquil waters are perfect for swimming, boating, and fishing, making it a favored spot for water sports aficionados. The surrounding area also offers well-maintained trails for hiking and cycling, providing stunning views of the lake and its natural surroundings. Picnic areas and designated barbecue spots around the lake make it a great location for family outings. Additionally, the nearby cafes and restaurants offer a taste of local cuisine, enhancing the visitor experience.

Getting There

Lake Mladost is conveniently located approximately 10 kilometers north of Veles. For those traveling from

Skopje, the capital city, the lake is about a one-hour drive via the E75/A1 motorway. To reach Lake Mladost, use the address: Lake Mladost, Veles 1400, North Macedonia, for GPS navigation. From Veles, visitors can take a taxi or drive via the local road that leads directly to the lake. Public transport options are also available, with local buses operating routes to the area.

A visit to Lake Mladost promises a refreshing escape into nature, offering a mix of recreational activities and serene landscapes, making it a must-visit destination in North Macedonia.

City Park Gevgelija
City Park Gevgelija, nestled in the heart of Gevgelija, North Macedonia, is a charming green oasis that offers a peaceful retreat from the bustling town. This well-maintained park provides a perfect spot for relaxation, family outings, and leisurely strolls amidst beautiful natural surroundings.

Attractions and Activities
City Park Gevgelija is adorned with lush lawns, vibrant flower beds, and shady trees, creating a serene environment for visitors. The park features walking paths, benches, and picnic areas, making it an ideal location for a tranquil afternoon. For families, there are playgrounds where children can enjoy various activities. Additionally, the park hosts occasional cultural events and local festivities, adding a touch of community spirit to the serene atmosphere.

Getting There

City Park Gevgelija is conveniently located at Marshal Tito Street, Gevgelija 1480, North Macedonia. For those traveling from Skopje, the capital city, Gevgelija is approximately a 90-minute drive via the A1 motorway. Regular bus and train services connect Skopje to Gevgelija, making public transport a convenient option. Once in Gevgelija, the park is easily accessible by foot from the town center. Visitors can also opt for local taxis, which provide a quick and easy way to reach the park.

Ohrid Museum

Ohrid Museum, located in the historic town of Ohrid, North Macedonia, is a treasure trove of cultural and historical artifacts that offer a glimpse into the rich heritage of the region. The museum is housed in several locations, each showcasing different aspects of Ohrid's illustrious past, from ancient times to the Ottoman period.

Attractions and Activities

The museum's primary exhibits are found in the Robev Family House, a beautifully preserved example of traditional Ottoman architecture. Visitors can explore various rooms filled with artifacts, including ancient coins, jewelry, and pottery, as well as religious icons and manuscripts. The ethnographic section provides insight into the traditional lifestyles and customs of the local people. Additionally, the museum complex includes the ancient Greek theater and the Church of St. Sophia, both of which are integral parts of Ohrid's cultural landscape.

Getting There

Ohrid Museum is centrally located at 2 Tsar Samuel Street, Ohrid 6000, North Macedonia. Ohrid is well-connected by road, with regular bus services from Skopje and other major cities. The journey from Skopje to Ohrid takes approximately three hours by bus or car. Once in Ohrid, the museum is easily accessible on foot from the town center. For visitors using GPS, the address is 2 Tsar Samuel Street, Ohrid 6000, North Macedonia. Local taxis are also available for those who prefer a quicker mode of transportation.

Struga Museum

Struga Museum, situated in the picturesque town of Struga, North Macedonia, offers a comprehensive look into the rich cultural and historical heritage of the region. The museum is renowned for its diverse collection of artifacts that span various periods, providing visitors with an in-depth understanding of Struga's past and its significance in Macedonian history.

Attractions and Activities

The museum is housed in a historic building that itself is a testament to the architectural styles of the region. Inside, visitors will find a wide array of exhibits, including archaeological finds, ethnographic displays, and artworks. The museum's archaeological section features artifacts from prehistoric, ancient, and medieval periods, highlighting the long history of human settlement in the area. The ethnographic section offers a glimpse into the traditional lifestyles, clothing, and crafts of the local people. Additionally, the museum often hosts temporary exhibitions and cultural events, further enriching the visitor experience.

Getting There

Struga Museum is conveniently located at 77 Kej Boris Kidric Street, Struga 6330, North Macedonia. Struga is accessible by road from major cities such as Skopje and Ohrid. From Skopje, the journey by car or bus takes approximately two and a half hours. Ohrid is much closer, with a travel time of about 20 minutes by car or bus. Once in Struga, the museum is within walking distance from the town center. For those using GPS, the address is 77 Kej Boris Kidric Street, Struga 6330, North Macedonia. Local taxis are also available and provide a convenient option for reaching the museum from any part of the town.

Galicica National Park

Galicica National Park, nestled between the stunning Lake Ohrid and Lake Prespa, is one of North Macedonia's natural treasures. This expansive park offers breathtaking landscapes, rich biodiversity, and a plethora of outdoor activities that attract nature enthusiasts and adventure seekers alike.

Attractions and Activities

Galicica National Park spans over 22,750 hectares, encompassing lush forests, rolling hills, and alpine meadows. The park is home to a diverse range of flora and fauna, including several endemic species. Visitors can explore numerous hiking and biking trails that offer panoramic views of the lakes and surrounding mountains. Popular activities include bird watching, as the park is a habitat for many rare bird species, and guided tours that provide insights into the park's unique ecosystem and cultural heritage. Additionally, the park features several archaeological sites and traditional mountain villages that add a cultural dimension to the natural beauty.

Getting There

Galicica National Park is located in southwestern North Macedonia, with its main entrance situated near the town of Ohrid. To reach the park, travelers can fly into Ohrid St. Paul the Apostle Airport, which is approximately 10 kilometers from the town center. From Ohrid, visitors can take a short drive along the E65 road, heading south towards St. Naum Monastery. The park's main entrance is well-signposted and lies along this route. For those using public transportation, buses from Ohrid to nearby villages like Trpejca and Ljubanishta provide access to different sections of the park. Taxis and rental cars are also convenient options for reaching the park and exploring its various attractions.

Galicica National Park offers an unforgettable experience, blending natural beauty, outdoor adventure, and cultural exploration. Its accessibility from Ohrid makes it a must-visit destination for anyone traveling to North Macedonia.

Ohrid Lake Promenade

The Ohrid Lake Promenade is a captivating destination in North Macedonia, offering a delightful blend of scenic beauty and vibrant local culture. Stretching along the shores of Lake Ohrid, this picturesque promenade is a hub for tourists and locals alike, providing a perfect setting for leisurely walks, dining, and relaxation.

Attractions and Activities

The promenade is lined with charming cafes, restaurants, and shops, where visitors can enjoy local cuisine, shop for souvenirs, or simply take in the stunning lake views. The area is also dotted with historical landmarks, including the ancient Church of St. Sophia and the Ohrid Fortress, which add a rich historical context to the serene landscape. During the summer months, the promenade buzzes with activity, hosting various cultural events, street performances, and open-air markets. Visitors can also rent bicycles or boats to explore the lake further or take a dip in the crystal-clear waters at one of the many lakeside beaches.

Getting There

To reach the Ohrid Lake Promenade, travelers can fly into Ohrid St. Paul the Apostle Airport, which is located about 10 kilometers from the town center. From the airport, taxis and shuttle services are readily available to transport visitors to the promenade area. For those traveling by bus, Ohrid is well-connected to other major cities in North Macedonia, with regular bus services operating from Skopje, Bitola, and other regions. Once in Ohrid, the promenade is easily accessible on foot from most parts of the town. It is centrally located, just a short walk from the main square and many of the town's hotels and guesthouses. Visitors driving to Ohrid can follow the E65 highway, with ample parking options available near the lakefront.

The Ohrid Lake Promenade offers a serene and culturally enriching experience, making it a highlight of any visit to North Macedonia. Its easy accessibility and wealth of attractions ensure that it remains a favorite spot for both relaxation and exploration.

Museum of Vinica

The Museum of Vinica, located in the heart of the town of Vinica, is a significant cultural and historical institution in North Macedonia. This museum offers visitors a fascinating glimpse into the rich heritage of the region, showcasing artifacts and exhibits that span various historical periods.

Exhibits and Collections

The museum is renowned for its collection of early Christian terracotta reliefs, known as the Vinica Tablets. These artifacts date back to the 4th to 6th centuries and are unique examples of early Christian art in the Balkans. In addition to the tablets, the museum houses a diverse range of archaeological finds, including pottery, tools, and coins, which provide insights into the daily lives and cultures of the ancient inhabitants of the area. The museum also features exhibits on the medieval period and the Ottoman era, offering a comprehensive overview of the region's history.

Getting There

To visit the Museum of Vinica, travelers can take a bus from Skopje, the capital of North Macedonia, which is approximately 100 kilometers away. Regular bus services connect Skopje to Vinica, making it a convenient and accessible destination. Once in Vinica, the museum is centrally located at Marshal Tito Street, easily reachable on foot from the town center. For those driving, Vinica can be accessed via the A3 highway from Skopje, with the journey taking around an hour and a half. There is ample parking available near the museum for those traveling by car.

The Museum of Vinica is a must-visit for history enthusiasts and those interested in the cultural heritage of North Macedonia. Its impressive collections and convenient location make it an enriching and accessible destination for all visitors.

Kochani Museum

Kochani Museum, situated in the town of Kochani, serves as a significant repository of the region's cultural and historical heritage. This museum offers visitors an in-depth look at the area's rich past through its diverse exhibits and collections.

Exhibits and Collections

The museum's exhibits span various periods, from prehistoric times to the modern era. Noteworthy among its collections are archaeological artifacts, including pottery, tools, and coins that illustrate the daily lives and customs of ancient civilizations that once thrived in the region. The museum also features ethnographic displays that provide insights into traditional Macedonian culture, showcasing traditional clothing, household items, and agricultural tools. These exhibits highlight the cultural continuity and evolution of the local population over the centuries.

Getting There

To visit Kochani Museum, travelers can take a bus from Skopje, the capital city of North Macedonia, which is approximately 120 kilometers away. Regular bus services connect Skopje to Kochani, making it a convenient destination. The museum is located at Nikola Karev Street, a central location in Kochani, easily reachable on foot from the town center. For those driving, Kochani can be accessed via the A3 and M5 highways from Skopje, with the journey taking around two hours. Adequate parking is available near the museum for those arriving by car.

Kochani Museum offers a rich and comprehensive exploration of the area's historical and cultural legacy, making it a valuable destination for history enthusiasts and cultural explorers alike. Its convenient location and diverse exhibits make it an essential stop on any visit to North Macedonia.

Berovo Lake

Berovo Lake, nestled in the Maleshevo Mountains in the eastern part of North Macedonia, is a picturesque destination known for its serene waters and lush surrounding forests. This artificial lake, created by damming the Bregalnica River, has become a popular spot for both relaxation and outdoor activities.

Scenic Beauty and Activities

Berovo Lake offers a tranquil setting ideal for picnicking, hiking, and fishing. The clear waters are perfect for swimming during the warmer months, while the surrounding trails invite visitors to explore the natural beauty of the region. Bird watching is also popular here, with numerous species inhabiting the area. The lake's peaceful ambiance makes it a perfect escape from the hustle and bustle of city life, providing a serene retreat in nature.

Getting There

To reach Berovo Lake, travelers typically start from Skopje, the capital of North Macedonia. The journey by car takes approximately three hours, covering a distance of about 160 kilometers. From Skopje, head southeast on the A1 highway towards Veles. Continue on the E75 and M5 roads, following signs for Berovo. Once in Berovo, the lake is about a 7-kilometer drive from the town center, accessible via the R5234 road. Adequate parking is available near the lake for those traveling by car.

For those using public transportation, buses run regularly from Skopje to Berovo. Upon arrival in Berovo, taxis or local transport can take you to the lake. The address for Berovo Lake is near the village of Ratevo, close to the town of Berovo. Signage along the route makes navigation straightforward.

City Park Stip

City Park Štip, located in the heart of Štip, is a vibrant and scenic public space that offers a refreshing retreat for both residents and visitors. This well-maintained park is a hub of recreational activities and a serene spot for relaxation amidst lush greenery and well-designed landscapes.

Features and Activities

City Park Štip boasts a variety of features that cater to different interests. There are walking and jogging paths, playgrounds for children, and numerous benches and picnic areas. The park is also home to beautiful flower beds, fountains, and small lakes, making it a picturesque location for leisurely strolls and nature appreciation. Additionally, it hosts various cultural events and community gatherings throughout the year, adding to its lively atmosphere.

Getting There

Reaching City Park Štip is straightforward whether you're traveling by car or using public transportation. Štip is approximately 90 kilometers southeast of Skopje, the capital of North Macedonia. By car, the journey takes around one and a half hours via the A3 highway. Once in Štip, the park is centrally located, making it easily accessible from different parts of the city.

For those using public transport, buses run frequently from Skopje to Štip. Upon arrival at the Štip bus station, the park is a short walk or taxi ride away. The address of City Park Štip is "Gradski Park Štip, 2000 Štip, North Macedonia." Clear signage and well-marked routes within the city guide visitors to the park.

City Park Štip offers a perfect blend of natural beauty and recreational facilities, making it a must-visit destination for anyone exploring Štip. Whether you're looking to relax, exercise, or enjoy community events, this park provides a welcoming environment for all.

CHAPTER TEN

MAJOR LANDMARKS AND HISTORICAL SITES

North Macedonia is rich in history and cultural heritage, evident in its numerous landmarks and historical sites scattered across various regions. Below is a comprehensive guide to the major landmarks and historical sites in each region, along with their addresses.

Skopje Region

Skopje Fortress (Kale)
Address: Old Town, Skopje, North Macedonia
This medieval fortress offers panoramic views of Skopje and is a significant historical monument, showcasing artifacts from various periods.

Stone Bridge
Address: Across the Vardar River, Skopje, North Macedonia
A symbol of Skopje, this historic bridge connects the old and new parts of the city and dates back to the Ottoman period.

Mother Teresa Memorial House
Address: Macedonian Str., Skopje, North Macedonia
Dedicated to Skopje's most famous resident, this site commemorates the life and work of Mother Teresa.
Pelagonia Region

Heraclea Lyncestis
Address: Near Bitola, Pelagonia Region, North Macedonia
An ancient city founded by Philip II of Macedon, featuring well-preserved mosaics, a Roman theater, and other ruins.

Bitola Museum
Address: Kliment Ohridski St., Bitola, North Macedonia
Housed in a former military academy, this museum covers the rich history and culture of Bitola and its surroundings.

Vardar Region
Stobi Archaeological Site
Address: Near Gradsko, Vardar Region, North Macedonia
One of the most significant archaeological sites in North Macedonia, showcasing ruins from the Hellenistic to the Roman period.

Tikveš Lake
Address: Near Kavadarci, Vardar Region, North Macedonia
A beautiful artificial lake surrounded by vineyards, with historical significance dating back to the early 20th century.

Southwestern Region
Ohrid Old Town
Address: Ohrid, Southwestern Region, North Macedonia
A UNESCO World Heritage Site, renowned for its ancient churches, traditional architecture, and Ohrid Lake.

Saint Naum Monastery
Address: Near Ohrid, Southwestern Region, North Macedonia
A historical monastery situated on the shores of Lake Ohrid, known for its beautiful frescoes and serene environment.

Eastern Region
Kokino Megalithic Observatory
Address: Near Kumanovo, Eastern Region, North Macedonia
An ancient observatory dating back to the Bronze Age, recognized as one of the oldest in the world.

Vinica Fortress
Address: Vinica, Eastern Region, North Macedonia
A medieval fortress offering insights into the region's historical defenses and stunning views of the surrounding area.

Southeastern Region
Strumica Fortress
Address: Strumica, Southeastern Region, North Macedonia

A medieval fortress with historical significance, providing a glimpse into the region's past military architecture.

Vodocha Monastery
Address: Near Strumica, Southeastern Region, North Macedonia
An important religious site with a rich history dating back to the Byzantine era.

Skopje Fortress (Kale)

Perched majestically on a hill overlooking the Vardar River, Skopje Fortress, commonly known as Kale, is one of North Macedonia's most iconic historical landmarks. This imposing fortress dates back to the 6th century, with its robust walls and towers having witnessed the rise and fall of various empires, including Byzantine, Ottoman, and Yugoslav influences.

The fortress offers a fascinating glimpse into the region's tumultuous past, with archaeological excavations revealing artifacts from various periods, including medieval and Roman times. The panoramic views from the top of the fortress are breathtaking, providing a sweeping vista of Skopje and its surroundings.

Getting There

Skopje Fortress is conveniently located in the heart of Skopje, making it easily accessible from various parts of the city. To reach the fortress, follow these directions:

By Foot: From the city center, you can enjoy a pleasant 15-minute walk. Start at Macedonia Square and head towards the Stone Bridge, which spans the Vardar River. Once you cross the bridge, continue straight along Samoilova Street, and you will see the fortress entrance on your right.

By Public Transport: Several bus lines stop near the fortress. Take buses number 2, 5, or 57 and alight at the "Bit Pazar" bus stop. From there, it's a short walk to the fortress entrance.

By Taxi: Taxis are readily available throughout Skopje. A taxi ride from the city center to the fortress should take about 5-10 minutes, depending on traffic.

Address: Old Town, Skopje, North Macedonia

Stone Bridge

The Stone Bridge, or "Kamen Most," is a remarkable architectural landmark in Skopje, North Macedonia. Spanning the Vardar River, this iconic bridge connects Macedonia Square with the Old Bazaar, serving as a symbolic and physical link between the city's modern and historic districts. Constructed in the 15th century during the reign of Sultan Mehmed II, the bridge showcases Ottoman engineering prowess with its robust stone arches and enduring design.

Walking across the Stone Bridge, you can enjoy splendid views of Skopje, capturing both the contemporary skyline and the historic charm of the Old Bazaar. The bridge is not only a vital pedestrian thoroughfare but also a site of historical significance, having survived numerous restorations and standing as a testament to Skopje's resilient spirit.

Getting There

Reaching the Stone Bridge is straightforward due to its central location:

By Foot: If you are in the city center, the bridge is easily accessible. From Macedonia Square, simply walk towards the river. The Stone Bridge is directly ahead, connecting you to the Old Bazaar on the other side.

By Public Transport: Several bus lines stop near Macedonia Square, such as buses number 3, 5, and 15. Alight at the "Macedonia Square" stop, then proceed to walk towards the river where you will find the bridge.

By Taxi: Taxis are plentiful in Skopje. A short ride from most central locations to the bridge should take only a few minutes. Ask the driver to drop you at Macedonia Square, from where the bridge is a short walk away.

Address: Between Macedonia Square and the Old Bazaar, Skopje, North Macedonia

Mother Teresa Memorial House

The Mother Teresa Memorial House in Skopje, North Macedonia, stands as a tribute to one of the most revered humanitarians of the 20th century, Mother Teresa. Born in Skopje in 1910, Mother Teresa dedicated her life to helping the poor and sick, eventually earning the Nobel Peace Prize in 1979. This memorial house, constructed near her birthplace, offers an intimate look into her life and legacy.

The memorial house, opened in 2009, features a museum with personal artifacts, photographs, and documents that trace Mother Teresa's journey from Skopje to her global humanitarian efforts. The site also includes a chapel where visitors can reflect and pay their respects. The building itself is a blend of traditional and modern architectural styles, symbolizing the timeless impact of Mother Teresa's work.

Getting There

The Mother Teresa Memorial House is conveniently located in the heart of Skopje, making it easily accessible from various points in the city.

By Foot: If you are staying in the city center, the memorial house is a short walk from Macedonia Square. Head west along Macedonia Street, and you will find the site on your left, near the intersection with Philip II of Macedonia Street.

By Public Transport: Several bus lines, including numbers 5, 15, and 19, pass close to the memorial house. Alight at the "Macedonia Square" stop and walk a few minutes west along Macedonia Street.

By Taxi: Taxis are readily available throughout Skopje. Request the driver to take you to the Mother Teresa Memorial House or to the intersection of Macedonia Street and Philip II of Macedonia Street.

Address: Macedonia Street, Skopje 1000, North Macedonia

Heraclea Lyncestis

Heraclea Lyncestis, an ancient city founded by Philip II of Macedon in the 4th century BC, is a remarkable archaeological site located near Bitola, North Macedonia. This historic site is renowned for its well-preserved mosaics, Roman baths, and a grand theater, offering a fascinating glimpse into the region's classical past.

Heraclea Lyncestis flourished during the Hellenistic period and later under Roman rule. Visitors can explore the remnants of its urban layout, including the intricate floor mosaics depicting various mythological scenes, which are among the finest in the Balkans. The Roman theater, constructed in the 2nd century AD, is another highlight, showcasing the architectural grandeur of the era. The site also includes basilicas with beautiful mosaics and frescoes that reflect the city's early Christian influence.

Getting There

Heraclea Lyncestis is situated approximately 2 kilometers south of Bitola, making it easily accessible from the city center.

By Car: If you are driving, take the road from Bitola towards Ohrid. Heraclea Lyncestis is signposted and lies just off this main road. Parking is available near the site entrance.

By Taxi: Taxis are a convenient option from Bitola. A short taxi ride will bring you directly to the entrance of Heraclea Lyncestis. Ensure to confirm the fare with the driver before starting the journey.

By Public Transport: Local buses from Bitola may also take you close to the site. Check with local bus services for routes that stop near Heraclea Lyncestis.

Address: Heraclea Lyncestis, Bitola 7000, North Macedonia

Stobi Archaeological Site

The Stobi Archaeological Site is one of North Macedonia's most significant and well-preserved ancient cities. Located near the confluence of the Crna and Vardar rivers, Stobi was an important urban center during the Roman and early Byzantine periods. Visitors can explore impressive remains, including a theater, basilicas, and intricate mosaics.

Stobi's origins date back to the 7th century BC, but it reached its peak during the Roman era, becoming a crucial hub on the Via Egnatia road. The site boasts an array of notable structures such as the Theater, which dates to the 2nd century AD, capable of seating over 7,000 spectators. The Baptistery with its striking mosaics, the Episcopal Basilica, and the luxurious Palaces of Theodosius are among the highlights, offering insights into the city's rich history and culture.

Getting There

Stobi is conveniently located near the village of Gradsko in central North Macedonia, making it accessible from major cities like Skopje and Bitola.

By Car: From Skopje, take the A1/E75 highway south towards Gradsko. The site is well-signposted and located approximately 80 kilometers from Skopje. Parking is available on-site.

By Bus: Regular buses operate from Skopje and Bitola to the nearby town of Gradsko. From Gradsko, local taxis or a short walk will bring you to the archaeological site.

By Train: The nearest train station is in Gradsko, with connections from major cities. From the station, you can take a taxi or walk to the site.

Address: Stobi Archaeological Site, Gradsko 1420, North Macedonia

Tikveš Lake

Tikveš Lake, the largest artificial lake in North Macedonia, is a stunning destination known for its beautiful scenery and rich biodiversity. The lake, created by the construction of the Tikveš Dam on the Crna River, is located in the Tikveš region, an area famed for its wine production. Surrounded by rolling hills and vineyards, Tikveš Lake offers a peaceful retreat for nature lovers and outdoor enthusiasts.

The lake is a haven for birdwatching, with numerous species of birds, including rare and endangered ones, inhabiting the area. Visitors can also enjoy a variety of activities such as fishing, boating, and hiking along the picturesque trails that surround the lake. The tranquil waters and scenic views make Tikveš Lake an ideal spot for picnics and relaxation.

Getting There

Tikveš Lake is easily accessible from several major cities in North Macedonia.

By Car: From Skopje, take the A1/E75 highway south towards Kavadarci. From Kavadarci, follow the signs to Tikveš Lake. The lake is approximately 110 kilometers from Skopje, making it about a 1.5-hour drive. There is parking available near the lake.

By Bus: Regular buses operate from Skopje and other major cities to Kavadarci. From Kavadarci, local transportation options such as taxis or buses can take you to the lake.

By Train: The nearest train station is in the town of Negotino, located approximately 20 kilometers from Tikveš Lake. From Negotino, you can take a taxi or a local bus to reach the lake.

Address: Tikveš Lake, near Kavadarci, North Macedonia

Ohrid Old Town

Ohrid Old Town, a UNESCO World Heritage site, is renowned for its rich history, stunning architecture, and picturesque location on the shores of Lake Ohrid. The town's ancient cobblestone streets are lined with well-preserved houses, Byzantine churches, and historical landmarks, offering visitors a glimpse into its storied past. Ohrid Old Town is a cultural treasure trove, attracting tourists with its blend of history, art, and natural beauty.

Key Attractions

Church of St. John at Kaneo: Perched on a cliff overlooking Lake Ohrid, this iconic church is known for its stunning views and beautiful frescoes.

Samoil's Fortress: Offering panoramic views of the town and lake, this ancient fortress is a must-visit for history enthusiasts.

Ancient Theatre of Ohrid: This well-preserved Hellenistic theatre hosts cultural events and performances, adding to the town's vibrant atmosphere.

Getting There

Ohrid Old Town is easily accessible from various parts of North Macedonia and beyond.

By Air: The closest airport is Ohrid St. Paul the Apostle Airport, located about 10 kilometers from the town center. From the airport, you can take a taxi or shuttle service to reach the old town.

By Car: If you are driving from Skopje, take the A2/E65 highway towards Ohrid. The journey is approximately 170 kilometers and takes around 2.5 hours. There are several parking areas near the old town.

By Bus: Regular bus services operate from Skopje and other major cities to Ohrid. The bus station is located about 1.5 kilometers from the old town, and you can reach the town center by taxi or a leisurely walk.

By Train: While there is no direct train service to Ohrid, you can take a train to Bitola and then a bus or taxi to Ohrid, which is about 70 kilometers away.

Address: Ohrid Old Town, Ohrid, North Macedonia

Saint Naum Monastery

Saint Naum Monastery, located on the southeastern shore of Lake Ohrid in North Macedonia, is a renowned spiritual and cultural landmark. Established in the 10th century by Saint Naum, a disciple of Saints Cyril and

Methodius, the monastery is a testament to Byzantine architecture and Orthodox heritage.

To visit the monastery, travelers typically start from the town of Ohrid. From Ohrid, the most convenient route is to drive south along the E65 road, which offers a scenic journey along the lake. The distance is approximately 29 kilometers and takes about 40 minutes by car. Alternatively, for those who prefer public transportation, regular buses run from Ohrid to the monastery, offering an affordable and picturesque ride.

Upon arrival, visitors are greeted by the monastery's stunning setting, surrounded by lush greenery and the serene waters of Lake Ohrid. The complex includes the Church of Saints Naum, adorned with frescoes and icons, and the tranquil garden where peacocks roam freely. The site also provides breathtaking views of the lake and mountains, making it a popular spot for photography and relaxation.

Kokino Megalithic Observatory

Kokino Megalithic Observatory, a significant archaeological and astronomical site in North Macedonia, dates back to the Bronze Age. Located near the village of Kokino, it is renowned for its ancient observatory function, where early inhabitants tracked celestial events.

To reach Kokino, travelers typically start from Skopje, the capital city. From Skopje, you can drive northeast on the A2 motorway towards the town of Kumanovo, a journey of about 40 kilometers. From Kumanovo, follow the signs to the village of Kokino, which is approximately 35 kilometers further. The entire trip by car takes about an hour and a half. Alternatively, you can take a bus from Skopje to Kumanovo and then hire a local taxi or arrange for a guided tour to the observatory.

Upon arrival, visitors will find an impressive site situated at an altitude of 1,013 meters, offering panoramic views of the surrounding landscape. The observatory consists of stone markers and platforms that align with the sunrise on solstices and equinoxes, providing insight into the advanced astronomical knowledge of its creators.

Kokino is not only a place of historical and scientific interest but also a spot of natural beauty, making it a popular destination for both history enthusiasts and nature lovers. Whether by car or guided tour, reaching Kokino Megalithic Observatory is a rewarding journey to one of North Macedonia's most fascinating ancient sites.

Vinica Fortress

Vinica Fortress, an archaeological site rich in history, is situated near the town of Vinica in North Macedonia. This ancient fortress, dating back to the Roman and Byzantine periods, is renowned for its well-preserved mosaics and fortifications, offering a glimpse into the region's past.

To reach Vinica Fortress, begin your journey from Skopje, the capital city. The drive to Vinica takes approximately two hours, covering around 120 kilometers. Take the A1 motorway towards Veles, then continue on the E75 highway until you reach the turnoff for the town of Stip. From Stip, follow the regional road R1302 towards Vinica. Upon arriving in Vinica, signs will direct you to the fortress, which is located on a hill overlooking the town.

For those preferring public transportation, buses run regularly from Skopje to Vinica, making the journey straightforward. Once in Vinica, a short taxi ride or a pleasant walk will take you to the fortress site.

Vinica Fortress, perched atop a hill, provides not only historical insights but also stunning views of the surrounding landscape. The site features remnants of ancient walls, towers, and gates, alongside the famous Vinica terracotta reliefs, which depict various religious and mythological scenes.

Visitors can explore the ruins and enjoy the scenic vistas, making it a must-see destination for history enthusiasts and travelers seeking to experience the cultural heritage of North Macedonia. Whether by car or public transport, visiting Vinica Fortress is an accessible and enriching excursion.

Strumica Fortress

Strumica Fortress, also known as Czar's Towers, is a significant historical landmark located near the town of Strumica in southeastern North Macedonia. This ancient fortress, dating back to the Byzantine era, stands atop a hill offering panoramic views of the Strumica Valley and its surrounding areas.

To reach Strumica Fortress, you can start your journey from Skopje, the capital city. The drive to Strumica takes approximately two and a half hours, covering a distance of about 150 kilometers. Take the A1 motorway heading south towards Veles, then continue on the E75 highway towards Demir Kapija. From there, follow the signs directing you to Strumica via the regional road R1402. Once you arrive in Strumica, local signage will guide you to the fortress, located just a short drive from the town center.

For those utilizing public transportation, there are regular bus services from Skopje to Strumica. The bus journey typically takes around three hours. Upon arriving in Strumica, you can take a taxi or opt for a leisurely walk to the fortress.

Strumica Fortress is accessible via a winding path that leads up the hill. The hike is moderate and rewards visitors with breathtaking views of the valley below. The fortress itself features remnants of ancient walls, towers, and gates, reflecting its historical significance and strategic importance throughout the centuries.

Visitors to Strumica Fortress can explore the ruins and enjoy the scenic landscapes, making it a perfect destination for history buffs and nature enthusiasts alike.

Whether by car or bus, the journey to Strumica Fortress is straightforward and well worth the effort for those seeking to delve into North Macedonia's rich cultural heritage.

Vodocha Monastery

Vodocha Monastery, a historical gem in North Macedonia, is located near the town of Strumica in the southeastern part of the country. This monastery, dating back to the 11th century, is renowned for its remarkable architecture and significant religious history. It features beautiful frescoes and intricate stonework, making it a vital site for both religious pilgrims and history enthusiasts.

To visit Vodocha Monastery, you can begin your journey from Skopje, the capital of North Macedonia. The drive to Strumica takes approximately two and a half hours, covering a distance of about 150 kilometers. Follow the A1 motorway heading south towards Veles, then continue on the E75 highway towards Demir Kapija. From Demir Kapija, take the regional road R1402 to reach Strumica. Once in Strumica, Vodocha Monastery is about 5 kilometers west of the town center.

If you prefer public transportation, regular bus services operate between Skopje and Strumica. The bus journey typically takes around three hours. Upon arrival in Strumica, you can take a local taxi or arrange for a guided tour to Vodocha Monastery, as it is a short drive from the town.

Visitors can enjoy a scenic route to the monastery, with clear signs leading the way. The tranquil setting of Vodocha Monastery, surrounded by nature, provides a peaceful atmosphere for reflection and exploration. The monastery's church, dedicated to the Holy Mother of God, features exquisite frescoes and historical artifacts that offer a glimpse into its rich past.

Whether traveling by car or bus, reaching Vodocha Monastery is convenient and allows visitors to immerse themselves in the serene beauty and historical significance of this cherished site in North Macedonia.

CHAPTER EIEVEN

ENTERTAINMENT AND NIGHTLIFE

North Macedonia offers a vibrant and diverse entertainment and nightlife scene, blending modern venues with traditional cultural experiences. The capital city, Skopje, stands out as the epicenter of nightlife, boasting a variety of options that cater to all tastes.

Skopje's Nightlife

In Skopje, the nightlife thrives in areas such as the Old Bazaar and the city center. The Old Bazaar is particularly famous for its atmospheric bars and cafes, where visitors can enjoy a drink in historic surroundings. Modern clubs like Stanica 26 and Epicentar host local and international DJs, offering lively music and dance floors that keep revelers entertained until the early hours.

For a more relaxed evening, the Debar Maalo neighborhood is known for its trendy bars and restaurants. Here, visitors can enjoy craft cocktails, local wines, and a range of cuisines in a more laid-back setting.

Ohrid's Lakeside Appeal

Ohrid, known for its stunning lake, also offers a unique nightlife experience. During the summer months, the lakeside promenades come alive with beach bars and open-air clubs. Places like Cuba Libre Beach Bar and

Aquarius are popular spots where locals and tourists alike gather to enjoy music, dancing, and stunning views of Lake Ohrid.

Bitola's Cultural Vibe

Bitola, with its rich history and cultural heritage, offers a different kind of nightlife. The city's main pedestrian street, Širok Sokak, is lined with cafes, bars, and restaurants, providing a charming setting for evening strolls and socializing. The Manaki Brothers Film Festival, held annually in Bitola, also adds a cultural dimension to the city's entertainment scene.

Festivals and Events

Throughout the year, North Macedonia hosts numerous festivals and events that enhance its nightlife. The Skopje Jazz Festival, held every October, attracts international artists and jazz enthusiasts. Strumica Carnival, one of the largest carnivals in the Balkans, takes place in February and features vibrant parades, music, and street parties.

How to Get There

Most entertainment venues in Skopje and other major cities are easily accessible by public transportation or taxi. Skopje's public buses run frequently, and taxis are widely available and affordable. In Ohrid and Bitola, local taxis and walking are the best ways to navigate the nightlife spots.

Skopje's Nightlife

Skopje, the vibrant capital of North Macedonia, boasts a dynamic nightlife scene that caters to a variety of tastes and preferences. From lively nightclubs to cozy bars and atmospheric cafes, the city offers something for everyone.

Popular Nightlife Spots

Stanica 26

Address: Nikola Vapcarov 10, Skopje 1000, North Macedonia

How to Get There: Located in the heart of Skopje, Stanica 26 is easily accessible via taxi or public transport. It's just a short walk from the main city square, making it convenient for visitors staying in central hotels. The venue is known for hosting local and international DJs, providing a vibrant atmosphere with diverse music genres.

Epicentar

Address: Nikola Vapcarov 4, Skopje 1000, North Macedonia

How to Get There: Situated near Stanica 26, Epicentar is also centrally located and can be reached by a brief taxi ride or by walking from central Skopje. This club is famous for its energetic dance floors and eclectic music, attracting a youthful and lively crowd.

Old Bazaar

How to Get There: The Old Bazaar is a historical district in Skopje, located on the eastern bank of the Vardar

River. Visitors can reach it by walking from the Stone Bridge or taking a short taxi ride from the city center. The area is renowned for its traditional charm, with numerous bars and cafes nestled among ancient cobblestone streets. Enjoy a drink in a setting that blends history with contemporary nightlife.

Debar Maalo
How to Get There: Debar Maalo is a trendy neighborhood within walking distance from the city center. It is accessible via public buses or a short taxi ride. Known for its stylish bars and restaurants, this area offers a relaxed evening out with a selection of craft cocktails, local wines, and diverse cuisines.

Entertainment Venues
MKC (Youth Cultural Center)
Address: Gjorche Petrov b.b., Skopje 1000, North Macedonia
How to Get There: MKC is located near the Vardar River, a short taxi ride or walk from the central area. The venue hosts concerts, film screenings, and cultural events, making it a hub for Skopje's artistic and cultural scene.

Beerhouse An
Address: Kapan An, Old Bazaar, Skopje 1000, North Macedonia
How to Get There: Beerhouse An is situated in the Old Bazaar within the historic Kapan An inn. Visitors can reach it by a short walk from the Stone Bridge or a brief taxi ride. This traditional beerhouse offers a cozy

atmosphere with a wide selection of local and international beers.

Getting Around

Skopje's nightlife spots are generally concentrated in central areas, making them easily accessible by various means of transport. The city's public buses operate frequently and are an affordable option for getting around. Taxis are widely available and reasonably priced, offering a convenient way to reach different venues. Walking is also a pleasant option, especially in the city center where many nightlife attractions are located within close proximity to each other.

Ohrid's Lakeside Appeal

Ohrid, often referred to as the "Jerusalem of the Balkans," is renowned for its stunning lakeside charm and rich historical heritage. Nestled on the shores of Lake Ohrid, one of Europe's oldest and deepest lakes, this picturesque town offers a perfect blend of natural beauty and cultural treasures.

Attractions and Activities

Lake Ohrid

Address: Lake Ohrid, Ohrid 6000, North Macedonia
How to Get There: The lake is the central feature of the town and can be easily accessed from any part of Ohrid. Visitors can enjoy leisurely walks along the lakeside promenade, engage in water activities such as swimming,

boating, and kayaking, or simply relax on the numerous beaches that line the shore.

Saint Sophia Cathedral

Address: Tsar Samoil 88, Ohrid 6000, North Macedonia
How to Get There: Located in the heart of the old town, the cathedral is a short walk from the lakeside. Follow the signs from the main square or the waterfront. This ancient church, dating back to the 11th century, is a testament to Ohrid's Byzantine history and features remarkable frescoes and architectural design.

Ancient Theatre of Ohrid

Address: Kuzman Kapidan, Ohrid 6000, North Macedonia
How to Get There: The theatre is situated in the old town, a brief uphill walk from the lakefront. Follow the marked paths through the historical district to reach this well-preserved Hellenistic-era site, which offers stunning views of the town and lake.

Samuel's Fortress

Address: Samoil's Fortress, Ohrid 6000, North Macedonia
How to Get There: Perched on a hill overlooking the lake, the fortress can be accessed by walking through the old town and following the signs. The climb is steep but rewarding, offering panoramic views of Ohrid and the surrounding area. This medieval structure provides a glimpse into the town's strategic significance in the past.

Saint Naum Monastery

Address: Saint Naum, Ohrid 6000, North Macedonia
How to Get There: Located about 29 kilometers south of Ohrid, the monastery can be reached by car or bus along the main road following the lake's eastern shore. The scenic drive offers breathtaking views of Lake Ohrid. Alternatively, boat tours from the town center also provide a unique way to visit the monastery, which is known for its serene setting and beautiful frescoes.

How to Get There

Ohrid is accessible by various means of transportation:

By Air: Ohrid St. Paul the Apostle Airport (OHD) is located approximately 10 kilometers from the town center. Regular flights connect Ohrid with major European cities, making it a convenient entry point for international travelers. Taxis and shuttle services are available at the airport for easy transfer to the town.

By Road: Ohrid is well-connected by road, with regular bus services from Skopje and other major cities in North Macedonia. The drive from Skopje, the capital city, takes about 2.5 to 3 hours via the A2 and E65 highways. Car rentals are also an option for those who prefer to explore at their own pace.

By Boat: For a more scenic approach, boat tours from nearby towns along Lake Ohrid offer a leisurely way to reach Ohrid, with stunning views of the lake and surrounding mountains.

Bitola's Cultural Vibe

Bitola, known as the "City of Consuls," is a vibrant hub of culture and history in North Macedonia. It combines the elegance of its Ottoman heritage with a lively contemporary scene, making it a must-visit destination for those seeking a blend of the old and new.

Attractions and Activities

Širok Sokak (Wide Street)
Address: Širok Sokak, Bitola 7000, North Macedonia
How to Get There: This main pedestrian street runs through the heart of Bitola and is easily accessible by foot from any part of the town. It is lined with neoclassical buildings, cafes, restaurants, and shops, providing a perfect place to experience the local culture and daily life.

Heraclea Lyncestis
Address: Heraclea, Bitola 7000, North Macedonia
How to Get There: Located about 2 kilometers south of Bitola's city center, this ancient city can be reached by a short taxi ride or a pleasant walk. Follow the signs from the main road leading out of Bitola. This archaeological site dates back to the 4th century BC and features well-preserved Roman mosaics, baths, and a theater.

Bitola Museum
Address: Kliment Ohridski bb, Bitola 7000, North Macedonia

How to Get There: The museum is situated in the old army barracks, close to the city park. From Širok Sokak, it is a 10-minute walk. Follow the signs or ask locals for directions. The museum offers extensive exhibits on Bitola's history, including its role in the Balkan Wars and World War I.

Magnolia Square

Address: Magnolia Square, Bitola 7000, North Macedonia

How to Get There: Located at the end of Širok Sokak, this square is a central point in Bitola and can be easily reached by walking. The square is surrounded by historical buildings and features the statue of Philip II of Macedonia, providing a great spot for photos and people-watching.

Clock Tower (Saat Kula)

Address: Clock Tower, Bitola 7000, North Macedonia

How to Get There: The Clock Tower is a prominent landmark in the city center, near Magnolia Square. It is easily accessible on foot from Širok Sokak. The tower dates back to the Ottoman period and offers a glimpse into Bitola's past.

St. Demetrius Church

Address: St. Demetrius Church, Bitola 7000, North Macedonia

How to Get There: This church is located near the old bazaar, a short walk from the main pedestrian area. Follow the signs from Širok Sokak or ask locals for directions. Known for its impressive frescoes and architectural design, the church is a significant religious site in Bitola.

How to Get There

Bitola is accessible by various means of transportation:

By Air: The nearest airport is Ohrid St. Paul the Apostle Airport (OHD), approximately 70 kilometers away. From the airport, you can take a taxi or a bus to Bitola. The journey takes about 1.5 hours by car.

By Road: Bitola is well-connected by road. Regular bus services run from Skopje, Ohrid, and other major cities in North Macedonia. The drive from Skopje, the capital city, takes about 3 hours via the A1 and E65 highways. Car rentals are available for those who prefer to explore at their own pace.

By Train: Bitola has a train station with connections to Skopje and other towns. The train journey offers a scenic route through the Macedonian countryside and is a comfortable way to reach Bitola.

Festivals and Events

North Macedonia is a country rich in cultural heritage, and its festivals and events reflect its diverse traditions and vibrant spirit. The nation's calendar is filled with celebrations that highlight music, dance, art, and local customs, offering visitors a unique glimpse into Macedonian life.

Ohrid Summer Festival

Dates: July to August

Description: Held in the picturesque town of Ohrid, the Ohrid Summer Festival is a prestigious event featuring classical music, theater performances, and ballet. Artists from around the world perform in historical settings such as the Ancient Theatre and the Church of St. Sophia, creating an enchanting atmosphere.

Skopje Jazz Festival

Dates: October

Description: The Skopje Jazz Festival attracts jazz enthusiasts from across the globe. This event showcases a wide range of jazz styles and hosts internationally renowned musicians. Concerts are held at various venues throughout Skopje, offering an intimate setting for music lovers.

Strumica Carnival

Dates: February or March (during the week before Ash Wednesday)

Description: The Strumica Carnival is one of the most colorful and lively events in North Macedonia. Participants don elaborate costumes and masks, parading through the streets in a celebration rooted in pagan traditions. The carnival features music, dance, and a spirit of revelry that captivates both locals and visitors.

Galichnik Wedding Festival

Dates: July (weekend closest to July 12, St. Peter's Day)
Description: This unique festival in the village of Galichnik reenacts a traditional Macedonian wedding ceremony. The event includes traditional dances, music, and customs, offering a vivid portrayal of the country's cultural heritage. The festival is a living museum of Macedonian traditions and attracts numerous spectators.

May Opera Evenings

Dates: May
Description: Held in Skopje, the May Opera Evenings is a month-long celebration of opera, featuring performances by prominent local and international artists. The event takes place in the Macedonian Opera and Ballet, providing a grand stage for operatic masterpieces.

Ilinden Uprising Day (St. Elijah's Day)

Dates: August 2
Description: Ilinden Uprising Day commemorates the 1903 uprising against Ottoman rule and is a significant national holiday. Celebrations occur throughout the country, with a major event at the memorial complex in Krushevo, where cultural programs and speeches honor the historical significance of the day.

Macedonian Independence Day

Dates: September 8
Description: Independence Day marks North Macedonia's declaration of independence from Yugoslavia in 1991. The day is celebrated with various

events, including concerts, parades, and fireworks, especially in the capital city, Skopje. It's a patriotic day filled with national pride and festivities.

Tikvesh Grape Harvest Festival
Dates: September
Description: Located in the wine region of Tikvesh, this festival celebrates the grape harvest with wine tastings, traditional music, and folk dances. It's a joyous event that highlights North Macedonia's rich winemaking traditions and offers a festive atmosphere for visitors to enjoy local wines and culture.

Balkan Folklore Festival
Dates: June
Description: This festival, held in Ohrid, brings together folklore ensembles from the Balkans and beyond. Participants showcase traditional dances, music, and costumes, promoting cultural exchange and preserving folklore traditions. The event is a vibrant display of the region's cultural diversity.

Open Youth Theatre (MOT)
Dates: September
Description: The Open Youth Theatre in Skopje is an international theater festival that features avant-garde and experimental performances. It serves as a platform for young and emerging artists to present their work, fostering creativity and innovation in the performing arts.

CHAPTER TWELVE

SHOPPING AND MARKET

North Macedonia offers a delightful shopping experience that combines traditional markets with modern retail spaces. Whether you are looking for artisanal crafts, fresh produce, or contemporary fashion, the country provides a diverse array of shopping opportunities.

Traditional Markets

North Macedonia's traditional markets, known as bazaars, are bustling hubs of activity where visitors can immerse themselves in local culture. These markets are perfect for finding unique souvenirs, handmade crafts, and local delicacies.

Old Bazaar in Skopje

Location: Skopje
Description: The Old Bazaar in Skopje is one of the oldest and largest marketplaces in the Balkans, dating back to the Ottoman period. It is a labyrinth of narrow streets lined with shops selling everything from jewelry and antiques to textiles and spices. The bazaar is also home to numerous cafes and restaurants, where visitors can enjoy traditional Macedonian cuisine.

Bit Pazar

Location: Skopje

Description: Situated near the Old Bazaar, Bit Pazar is a vibrant market offering a variety of goods, including fresh produce, clothing, and household items. The market is known for its lively atmosphere and is a great place to experience the daily life of Skopje's residents.

Green Market

Location: Bitola

Description: The Green Market in Bitola is a popular destination for fresh fruits and vegetables, dairy products, and homemade goods. The market's stalls are filled with local farmers' produce, providing a true taste of Macedonian agriculture.

Modern Shopping Centers

For those seeking a more contemporary shopping experience, North Macedonia boasts several modern malls and shopping centers that cater to a variety of tastes and preferences.

Skopje City Mall

Location: Skopje

Description: Skopje City Mall is the largest shopping center in North Macedonia, offering a wide range of international and local brands. The mall features numerous retail stores, a food court, cinemas, and entertainment options, making it a one-stop destination for shopping and leisure.

Capitol Mall
Location: Skopje
Description: Located in the Aerodrom municipality, Capitol Mall combines retail shopping with dining and entertainment. It houses a variety of shops, including fashion boutiques, electronics stores, and a supermarket, along with cafes and a cinema.

Ramstore Mall
Location: Skopje
Description: Situated in the heart of Skopje, Ramstore Mall offers a blend of shopping and dining experiences. The mall includes a mix of high-end and affordable brands, as well as restaurants and cafes, providing a convenient spot for both locals and tourists.

Craft Shops and Boutiques
In addition to bazaars and malls, North Macedonia has numerous small craft shops and boutiques where visitors can purchase unique items and support local artisans.

Macedonian Handicrafts Shop
Location: Skopje
Description: This shop specializes in traditional Macedonian crafts, including handwoven textiles, pottery, and woodwork. It is an excellent place to find authentic souvenirs that reflect the country's rich cultural heritage.

Bitola Art Gallery and Craft Shop
Location: Bitola
Description: Located in the historic city of Bitola, this gallery and shop feature works by local artists and craftsmen. Visitors can purchase paintings, sculptures, and handmade jewelry, all showcasing the creativity of Macedonian artisans.

How to Get There
Skopje City Mall
Address: Ljubljanska 4, Skopje
Directions: Easily accessible by public transport, with several bus lines stopping nearby. Alternatively, it is a short taxi ride from the city center.

Old Bazaar, Skopje
Address: Čair, Skopje
Directions: Located within walking distance from the main square, accessible via public transport with numerous bus lines servicing the area.

Bitola Green Market
Address: Shirok Sokak, Bitola
Directions: Centrally located, it can be reached on foot from most parts of the city or by local bus.

local product and souvenirs
North Macedonia is a treasure trove of unique and culturally rich products that make perfect souvenirs. The

country's traditional crafts, culinary delights, and artisanal goods reflect its rich history and vibrant culture.

Traditional Handicrafts
Handwoven Textiles
Description: North Macedonia is renowned for its exquisite handwoven textiles, including carpets, rugs, and embroidered linens. These items are often crafted using traditional techniques passed down through generations, featuring intricate patterns and vibrant colors that tell stories of Macedonian folklore and heritage.

Woodcarvings
Description: The art of woodcarving is deeply rooted in Macedonian tradition. Artisans skillfully create intricate designs on various wooden objects, such as furniture, religious icons, and decorative items. Each piece is a testament to the craftsmanship and artistic expression unique to the region.

Pottery
Description: Macedonian pottery is celebrated for its distinctive shapes and decorative motifs. Local potters produce a wide range of ceramic items, including plates, bowls, and vases, often adorned with traditional patterns and glazes. These pieces make beautiful and functional souvenirs.

Filigree Jewelry
Description: Filigree is a delicate form of jewelry making that involves twisting fine threads of gold or silver into intricate designs. Macedonian filigree jewelry is highly prized for its elegance and craftsmanship, making it a perfect gift or keepsake.

Culinary Delights
Ajvar
Description: Ajvar is a delicious pepper-based condiment that is a staple in Macedonian cuisine. Made from roasted red peppers, garlic, and sometimes eggplant, ajvar can be enjoyed as a spread, dip, or side dish. It is often sold in jars, making it easy to take home and share a taste of Macedonia with friends and family.

Rakija
Description: Rakija is a traditional fruit brandy commonly consumed in North Macedonia. Made from various fruits, such as grapes, plums, or apricots, rakija is a popular spirit enjoyed during celebrations and social gatherings. Bottles of rakija make excellent souvenirs for those who appreciate fine spirits.

Wine
Description: North Macedonia is home to several renowned wine regions, producing high-quality wines that have gained international recognition. Local wines, particularly those made from indigenous grape varieties like Vranec and Smederevka, are excellent souvenirs for wine enthusiasts.

Artistic Souvenirs

Paintings and Icons

Description: Macedonian art is rich with religious and cultural themes. Paintings and icons, often depicting scenes from Orthodox Christianity or traditional life, are beautiful pieces to bring home. These artworks are typically available in galleries and specialized shops.

Macedonian Folk Costumes

Description: Traditional Macedonian folk costumes are intricately designed with colorful embroidery and patterns. While it might not be practical to purchase a full costume, smaller items like embroidered shirts, scarves, or belts can be wonderful souvenirs that capture the essence of Macedonian culture.

Specialty Shops and Markets

Old Bazaar, Skopje

Description: The Old Bazaar in Skopje is a vibrant marketplace where visitors can find a variety of traditional products and souvenirs. The bazaar's narrow streets are lined with shops selling textiles, jewelry, pottery, and other artisanal goods.

Bitola Green Market

Description: This market is a hub for local produce and handmade goods. It's an excellent place to purchase culinary souvenirs, such as ajvar, rakija, and other regional specialties.

Ohrid Shops

Description: The town of Ohrid is famous for its pearls and intricate silver filigree jewelry. Visitors can explore numerous shops offering these unique items, along with other local crafts and souvenirs.

How to Get There

Old Bazaar, Skopje

Address: Čair, Skopje
Directions: Located near the city center, the Old Bazaar is easily accessible by foot from the main square or via public transportation with multiple bus lines serving the area.

Bitola Green Market

Address: Shirok Sokak, Bitola
Directions: Situated in the heart of Bitola, this market can be reached on foot from most parts of the city or by using local buses.

Ohrid Shops

Address: Central Ohrid
Directions: The shops are located within walking distance of Ohrid's main attractions and can be easily accessed by foot or a short taxi ride.

CHAPTER THIRTEEN

PRACTICAL INFORMATION

When planning a visit to North Macedonia, having practical information at your fingertips can make your trip smoother and more enjoyable.

Visa and Passport

EU Citizens: European Union citizens can enter North Macedonia without a visa for stays of up to 90 days within a 180-day period.

Non-EU Citizens: Travelers from certain countries may require a visa. It is advisable to check with the Macedonian embassy or consulate in your home country for specific entry requirements.

Passport Validity: Ensure your passport is valid for at least six months beyond your intended departure date.

Air Travel

Main Airport: Skopje International Airport (SKP) is the primary gateway, located approximately 23 kilometers from the capital city.

Secondary Airport: Ohrid St. Paul the Apostle Airport (OHD) serves the southwestern region, offering seasonal flights.

Public Transport

Buses: An extensive network of intercity buses connects major towns and cities. In Skopje, the public bus system is the main mode of transportation.

Trains: While the rail network is less comprehensive, trains connect major cities like Skopje, Bitola, and Veles.

Car Rentals

Availability: Car rental services are widely available in major cities and at airports. Driving is on the right side of the road.

Currency

Macedonian Denar (MKD): The local currency is the Macedonian denar. Currency exchange services are available at airports, banks, and exchange offices.

Credit Cards: Major credit cards are widely accepted in hotels, restaurants, and shops. However, it is advisable to carry some cash, especially in rural areas.

ATMs

Availability: ATMs are plentiful in cities and towns, offering convenient access to cash withdrawals.

Official Language

Macedonian: The official language is Macedonian, written in the Cyrillic script.

Albanian: Albanian is also widely spoken, particularly in regions with significant Albanian communities.

Other Languages
English: English is commonly spoken in urban areas and tourist centers, especially by younger generations and in the hospitality industry.

German and French: These languages may also be understood in some tourist areas.

Health Care
Medical Services: North Macedonia has public and private healthcare facilities. Travelers are advised to have comprehensive travel insurance that covers medical expenses.

Pharmacies: Pharmacies are readily available in cities and towns, providing both prescription and over-the-counter medications.

Safety
General Safety: North Macedonia is considered safe for travelers. However, standard precautions should be taken to safeguard personal belongings.

Emergency Numbers: The general emergency number is 112. For specific services, dial 192 for police, 193 for fire, and 194 for medical emergencies.

Internet and Mobile
Wi-Fi: Free Wi-Fi is available in many hotels, cafes, and public areas.

SIM Cards: Local SIM cards can be purchased for mobile phone use, offering affordable data and call packages.

Voltage
Standard Voltage: The standard voltage is 230V, with a frequency of 50Hz. Power sockets are of type F (two round pins).

Time Zone
Central European Time (CET): North Macedonia operates on CET (UTC+1). Daylight Saving Time is observed, moving clocks forward one hour in the spring and back in the autumn.

Customary Practice
Restaurants and Cafes: Tipping around 10% of the bill is customary if service is not included.

Taxis and Hotels: Rounding up the fare or leaving a small tip for good service is appreciated.

In summary, North Macedonia offers a rich and accessible travel experience, with straightforward entry requirements, reliable transportation options, and essential services to ensure a comfortable stay. By being well-prepared with practical information, travelers can fully enjoy the diverse cultural and natural attractions this captivating country has to offer.

Packing Essentials

When planning your trip to North Macedonia, ensuring you have the right items in your luggage can significantly enhance your travel experience.

Seasonal Attire

Spring and Autumn: Pack layers, including light jackets, long-sleeve shirts, and trousers. These seasons can be unpredictable, with mild temperatures during the day and cooler evenings.

Summer: Light, breathable clothing is essential for the hot summer months. Include shorts, t-shirts, dresses, and swimwear. Don't forget a hat and sunglasses to protect against the strong sun.

Winter: If visiting in winter, pack warm clothing such as coats, sweaters, scarves, gloves, and thermal wear, especially if you plan to visit mountainous regions.

Footwear

Comfortable Walking Shoes: Essential for exploring cities, historical sites, and markets.

Hiking Boots: Necessary for outdoor activities, including trekking in national parks and mountainous areas.

Casual and Formal Shoes: Pack casual shoes for daily wear and a pair of formal shoes if you plan to dine in upscale restaurants or attend events.

Toiletries

Basic Toiletries: Include shampoo, conditioner, soap, deodorant, toothpaste, and toothbrush. While these items are available locally, it's convenient to have your preferred brands.

Sunscreen and Insect Repellent: Crucial for protection against the sun and insects, especially during outdoor activities.

Health and Medical Supplies

Prescription Medications: Bring enough of any necessary medications for the duration of your trip, along with a copy of your prescription.

First Aid Kit: Include band-aids, antiseptic wipes, pain relievers, and any other personal medical supplies.

Documents

Passport and Visa: Ensure your passport is valid for at least six months beyond your intended stay. Carry any necessary visas.

Travel Insurance: Bring proof of travel insurance that covers medical emergencies and trip cancellations.

Copies of Important Documents: Keep photocopies or digital copies of your passport, visa, travel insurance, and emergency contact information.

Technology

Mobile Phone and Charger: A mobile phone is essential for navigation, communication, and capturing memories.

Power Bank: Handy for keeping your devices charged during long days of exploration.

Camera: If you prefer high-quality photos, bring a camera along with extra memory cards and batteries.

Adapters and Converters

Power Adapter: North Macedonia uses type F power sockets (two round pins), and the standard voltage is 230V. Pack a suitable adapter if your devices have different plug types.

Voltage Converter: If your electronic devices do not support 230V, a voltage converter will be necessary.

Daypack or Backpack

For Daily Use: A small, comfortable backpack is useful for carrying daily essentials like water, snacks, a map, and a camera.

Reusable Water Bottle

Stay Hydrated: Carry a reusable water bottle to stay hydrated, especially during outdoor activities.

Snacks

Travel Snacks: Pack some non-perishable snacks like nuts, dried fruit, or granola bars for long journeys and day trips.

Modest Clothing

Respect Local Customs: When visiting religious sites and rural areas, pack modest clothing that covers shoulders and knees to respect local customs and traditions.

Technology and Connectivity

North Macedonia, while rich in history and natural beauty, is also progressively embracing modern technology and connectivity.

Wi-Fi Availability

North Macedonia offers widespread Wi-Fi access in urban centers, particularly in Skopje, Ohrid, and Bitola. Many hotels, cafes, restaurants, and public spaces provide free Wi-Fi for guests, ensuring that staying connected is convenient for travelers. The speed and reliability of these connections can vary, but major cities typically offer robust services.

Mobile Internet

For more reliable and on-the-go internet access, consider purchasing a local SIM card. Major telecommunications providers such as T-Mobile, A1, and Lycamobile offer prepaid SIM cards with various data plans, which are available at airports, major shopping centers, and retail stores. Ensure your phone is unlocked to use a local SIM card.

Network Coverage
North Macedonia has extensive mobile network coverage, particularly in urban areas and along major transportation routes. Rural and remote areas might experience weaker signals, but overall, the country has a well-developed mobile infrastructure.

International Roaming
Visitors can use their home country's mobile service through international roaming agreements. However, this option can be expensive. It is advisable to check with your mobile provider for international roaming rates and consider a local SIM card as a cost-effective alternative.

Public Telephones
While the use of public telephones has declined with the proliferation of mobile phones, they are still available in some urban locations. Public telephones accept phone cards, which can be purchased at post offices, kiosks, and convenience stores.

Electricity
North Macedonia uses the European standard voltage of 230V and a frequency of 50Hz. The power sockets are type F, with two round pins. Travelers from countries with different plug types should bring suitable adapters. It's also prudent to carry a voltage converter if your devices are not compatible with 230V.

Charging Stations

Many cafes, restaurants, and public spaces provide charging stations or outlets for customers to use. Portable power banks are also a handy accessory for keeping your devices charged during long days of sightseeing.

Online Safety

As with any travel destination, practicing good cyber hygiene is essential. Use secure Wi-Fi networks, avoid accessing sensitive information on public Wi-Fi, and consider using a VPN for added security.

Emergency Services

For immediate assistance, North Macedonia has a single emergency number: 112. This number connects to all emergency services, including police, medical, and fire departments.

Photography tips

North Macedonia, with its stunning landscapes, historic sites, and vibrant culture, offers a wealth of photographic opportunities.

Camera Equipment

To best capture North Macedonia's diverse scenery, consider bringing a versatile camera setup. A DSLR or mirrorless camera with interchangeable lenses will give you flexibility. A wide-angle lens is ideal for landscapes and architecture, while a telephoto lens is useful for wildlife and distant subjects.

Tripod

A sturdy tripod is invaluable for landscape photography, especially during low-light conditions such as sunrise and sunset. It also helps in stabilizing shots for long exposures and night photography.

Filters

Consider using polarizing filters to reduce glare and enhance the colors of the sky and water. Neutral density filters can be helpful for capturing long exposures, particularly when photographing waterfalls and rivers.

Golden Hours

The golden hours—shortly after sunrise and before sunset—provide the best lighting for photography. The soft, warm light during these times enhances landscapes and adds depth to your photos.

Blue Hour

The blue hour, which occurs just before sunrise and after sunset, offers a unique atmosphere with deep blue tones in the sky, perfect for capturing cityscapes and waterfronts.

Lake Ohrid

Lake Ohrid is a must-visit for any photographer. The clear blue waters, framed by mountains and historic architecture, provide stunning vistas. For the best shots, head to the Church of St. John at Kaneo, which offers panoramic views of the lake and town.

Matka Canyon

Matka Canyon, near Skopje, is another prime location. The dramatic cliffs, serene waters, and ancient monasteries make for compelling compositions. A boat trip down the Treska River offers unique perspectives and access to hidden spots.

Skopje's Old Bazaar

Skopje's Old Bazaar is rich in cultural and architectural details. Capture the vibrant street life, colorful market stalls, and historic buildings. Early morning and late afternoon are ideal times to avoid crowds and harsh midday light.

Pelister National Park

For nature and wildlife photography, Pelister National Park is a top destination. The park's diverse flora and fauna, along with its pristine landscapes, offer numerous photographic opportunities. The Big Lake and Small Lake, known as the Pelister Eyes, are particularly photogenic.

Respect Local Customs

When photographing people, always ask for permission first. This is particularly important in rural areas and at religious sites. Being respectful and polite will usually result in more natural and cooperative subjects.

Be Prepared for Weather Changes

North Macedonia's weather can be unpredictable, especially in mountainous regions. Dress in layers and bring weatherproof gear to protect your equipment from rain and dust.

Capture the Details
While landscapes and architecture are captivating, don't forget to capture the smaller details that tell the story of North Macedonia. Close-ups of traditional crafts, local cuisine, and everyday street scenes can add depth and context to your photographic narrative.

Editing
Post-processing is an essential part of digital photography. Use software like Adobe Lightroom or Photoshop to enhance your images, but be careful not to overdo it. Aim for natural-looking adjustments that reflect the true beauty of the scenes you captured.

Useful Websites and Apps
In today's digital age, having access to the right websites and apps can significantly enhance your travel experience in North Macedonia.

Official Tourism Portal
The official tourism website of North Macedonia (www.northmacedonia-timeless.com) offers comprehensive information on destinations, cultural events, accommodation, and travel tips. It's an excellent starting point for planning your trip. The website is user-friendly and regularly updated with the latest travel advisories and news.

Skopje City Guide

For detailed insights into the capital city, visit www.skopjecityguide.com. This site provides information on attractions, dining, shopping, and nightlife in Skopje. It also includes maps and suggested itineraries to help you make the most of your visit.

Macedonian Museum Network

If you are interested in exploring the rich history and culture of North Macedonia, the Macedonian Museum Network website (www.mmn.mk) is invaluable. It offers details on various museums, exhibitions, and heritage sites across the country. The website includes contact information, opening hours, and ticket prices.

My Macedonia

Available on both iOS and Android platforms, the My Macedonia app is a comprehensive travel guide that includes information on attractions, accommodations, restaurants, and events. The app features offline maps and GPS navigation, making it an essential tool for travelers without constant internet access. Download it from the App Store or Google Play.

Nextbike

For eco-friendly travel, the NextBike app allows you to rent bicycles in several Macedonian cities, including Skopje. The app provides real-time information on bike availability and station locations. You can easily register and pay through the app, making it a convenient option for exploring urban areas. Download it from the App Store or Google Play.

Moj Vodič

This app serves as a personal tour guide, offering audio guides and detailed information on key tourist sites in North Macedonia. Moj Vodič covers historical landmarks, museums, and natural wonders. The app's user-friendly interface allows you to select tours based on your interests and time availability. It's available for download on both iOS and Android devices.

Trafika.mk

For real-time traffic updates and navigation, Trafika.mk is an indispensable app. It provides information on road conditions, traffic jams, and alternative routes, helping you navigate the country efficiently. The app can be downloaded from the App Store or Google Play.

GetByBus

For intercity travel, the GetByBus app offers schedules, ticket booking, and route planning for buses across North Macedonia. The app is user-friendly and supports multiple languages, making it accessible for international travelers. It's available for download on iOS and Android platforms.

How to Access and Use

To get started, visit the respective websites or app stores (App Store for iOS devices and Google Play for Android devices). Search for the app by its name, and download and install it on your device. Most apps require a one-time registration process, where you provide basic information and set up payment methods if necessary. Once installed, these apps and websites provide intuitive interfaces to access the information and services you need, whether it's booking tickets, navigating cities, or discovering attractions.

Tourist Information Centers

Tourist information centers are invaluable resources for travelers, providing essential information, maps, and guidance to ensure a smooth and enriching visit. In North Macedonia, these centers are strategically located in key cities and tourist hotspots.

Skopje Tourist Information Center

Address: Macedonia Square, 1000 Skopje

Located in the heart of the capital, the Skopje Tourist Information Center is your go-to place for comprehensive information on the city and its surroundings. Here, you can find brochures, maps, and details on local attractions, events, and accommodations. The friendly staff can assist with travel arrangements and offer insightful recommendations to enhance your visit.

Ohrid Tourist Information Center

Address: Kosta Abrash 15, 6000 Ohrid

Situated in the picturesque town of Ohrid, this information center provides extensive resources on the region's historical sites, cultural events, and natural attractions. Visitors can obtain information on boat tours, hiking trails, and UNESCO World Heritage sites, ensuring a memorable experience in this stunning lakeside destination.

Bitola Tourist Information Center
Address: Shirok Sokak, 7000 Bitola

Located on the main pedestrian street of Bitola, the tourist information center offers valuable insights into the city's rich history and vibrant cultural scene. Here, you can get information on local museums, historical landmarks, and upcoming festivals. The center also provides maps and guides for exploring Bitola and its surroundings.

Tetovo Tourist Information Center
Address: Ilindenska, 1200 Tetovo

This center serves as a gateway to exploring the western region of North Macedonia. It offers detailed information on local attractions, including the Shar Mountain, the Painted Mosque, and traditional crafts. The staff can assist with travel plans, providing tips on accommodations and dining options in Tetovo and nearby areas.

Strumica Tourist Information Center
Address: Goce Delchev 12, 2400 Strumica

Situated in the southeastern part of the country, the Strumica Tourist Information Center offers resources on the region's natural beauty and cultural heritage. Visitors can learn about local festivals, historical sites, and outdoor activities such as hiking and exploring waterfalls. The center provides maps and travel guides to ensure a well-rounded visit.

Kumanovo Tourist Information Center
Address: Nikola Tesla 21, 1300 Kumanovo

This center provides information on the northern region of North Macedonia, including details on local attractions, events, and accommodations. The staff can assist with travel plans and offer recommendations for exploring Kumanovo and its surroundings, including archaeological sites and natural parks.

Prilep Tourist Information Center
Address: Makedonska Revolucija 3, 7500 Prilep

Located in central North Macedonia, the Prilep Tourist Information Center offers insights into the city's rich history and cultural events. Visitors can obtain information on local attractions, including monasteries, historical monuments, and traditional festivals. The center provides maps and travel guides to help you explore Prilep and the surrounding areas.

Services Offered

All tourist information centers in North Macedonia provide a range of services to assist travelers, including:

Distribution of brochures, maps, and travel guides.
Information on local attractions, events, and accommodations.

Assistance with travel arrangements and transportation options.

Recommendations on dining, shopping, and entertainment.

Multilingual staff to cater to international visitors.

How to Get There

Each tourist information center is conveniently located in central areas or near major tourist attractions, making them easily accessible by public transportation or on foot. Addresses provided above can be input into navigation apps for precise directions. Public transport information, including bus routes and schedules, is often available on local websites or directly at the centers.

MY PERSONAL NOTE

....
....
....
....
....
....
....
....
....
....
....
....
....
....
....
....
....
....
....
....
....
....
....
....
....
....
....

....
....
....
....
....
....
....
....
....
....
....
....
....
....
....
....
....
....
....
....
....
....
....
....
....
....
....
....
....
....
....

....
....
....
....
....
....
....
....
....
....
....
....
....
....
....
....
....
....
....
....
....
....
....
....
....
....
....
....
....
....
....
....
....
....

....
....
....
....
....
....
....
....
....
....
....
....
....
....
....
....
....
....
....
....
....
....
....
....
....
....
....
....
....
....
....
....
....

....
....
....
....
....
....
....
....
....
....
....
....
....
....
....
....
....
....
....
....
....
....
....
....
....
....
....
....

THANKS,WISH YOU SAFE TRAVEL.

Printed in Great Britain
by Amazon